Louis Felsenthal
*Citizen-Soldier of
Territorial New Mexico*

Capt. Louis Felsenthal, September 1865. Felsenthal was
stationed at Fort Union when this photograph was taken, but
he was making plans to return to civilian life. (Courtesy
Museum of New Mexico, Photo Collections)

Louis Felsenthal
Citizen-Soldier
of Territorial New Mexico

Jacqueline Dorgan Meketa

Published in cooperation
with the Historical Society
of New Mexico

University of New Mexico Press
Albuquerque

Library of Congress Cataloging in Publication Data

Meketa, Jacqueline
    Louis Felsenthal, citizen-soldier of territorial
New Mexico.

      Bibliography: p.
      Includes index.
      1. Felsenthal, Louis, 1832-1909. 2. Jews—New
Mexico—Santa Fe—Biography. 3. New Mexico—History
—Civil War, 1861-1865. 4. Santa Fe (N.M.)—
Biography. I. Historical Society of New Mexico.
II. Title
F804.S29J535   978.9′04′0924 [B]   82-2802
ISBN 0-8263-0619-5   AACR2
ISBN 0-8263-0604-7 (pbk.)

©1982 by the University of New Mexico Press
All rights reserved
Manufactured in the United States of America
Library of Congress Catalog Card Number 82-2802
International Standard Book Number 0-8263-0604-7 (paper)
0-8263-0619-5 (cloth)
First edition.

Dedicated
to my seven children,
in whom I have an unbounded pride

James, Michael, Richard,
Anthony, Robert, Thomas,
and Rebecca

Contents

Illustrations

Maps

Foreword

The Historical Society of New Mexico is pleased to cosponsor Jacqueline Dorgan Meketa's LOUIS FEL-SENTHAL, CITIZEN-SOLDIER OF TERRITORIAL NEW MEXICO as the second title in the joint-publication program between the Society and the University of New Mexico Press. The purpose of the history series is to publish works on New Mexico, emphasizing those areas and topics that have not been dealt with or those which need up-dating or reprinting. This volume on Louis Felsenthal is in the category of publishing on a topic that has not been covered previously. It is the history of a Jewish immigrant to New Mexico, and as such tells us much about the daily life of a group that until now has not received the study it deserves.

This book is at once a biography of Felsenthal and an account of the life of a representative figure of the Territorial Period in New Mexico. His years in New Mexico—from 1858 to 1902—and his experiences in business, politics, law, and soldiering are reconstructed in rich and fascinating detail by Meketa. Felsenthal is of particular interest to the Society for one other reason: he was instrumental in the founding of our organization.

The publication program of the Society and the arrangement with the University of New Mexico Press enable both groups to achieve important goals: for the Society, to increase the research and writings of New Mexico history; for the Press, to contribute to the development and enjoyment of our regional culture.

The 1981 officers and directors are: *Officers:* Albert H. Schroeder, President; John P. Conron, Vice President; Austin Hoover, 2nd Vice President; Mrs. Hedy M. Dunn, Secretary; and Charles Bennett, Treasurer. *Directors:* Jack K. Boyer, Thomas E. Chavez, Timothy Cornish, Octavia Fellin, Dr. Myra Ellen Jenkins, Loraine Lavender, Luther L. Lyon, Morgan Nelson, Mrs. George G. Otero, Mrs. Gordon Robertson, Joe W. Stein, Michael F. Weber, Dr. Spencer Wilson, and Stephen Zimmer.

John P. Conron, Chairman
Publications Committee
Historical Society of New Mexico

Preface

For years I have been an avid reader of biographies, but I did not think that my own writing might take as its subject the reconstruction of the life of a person I knew only through documents. It was not until I realized that the research notes I had accumulated for five years contained abundant and rich material that enabled me to piece together the career of a nineteenth century citizen-soldier of Territorial New Mexico that I undertook to write the biography of Louis Felsenthal.

Much of my work on Louis Felsenthal has been in the nature of historian-detective, and this was especially true early on. I became interested in Louis Felsenthal as a result of a discussion of a research problem with my husband. He casually mentioned that evening in the spring of 1974 that I might want to investigate the background of a man whose name was engraved on a silver plaque attached to a rifle he had owned for more than twenty years. My husband recalled that in the 1950s an Albuquerque newspaper reporter, knowledgeable in New Mexico history, had made a cursory search for information about the former owner of the antique gun; his efforts were unsuccessful.

I began with no more information than that incorporated in the brief inscription on the shield-shaped insert, "Louis Felsenthal, Captain, 1st N. M. Inf." I used the Maynard rifle as the first clue in my investigation, for by researching its date of manufacture in a firearms catalog, I was able to determine the period in which it was most likely to have been a weapon of value and utility to a military officer. The carbine, I discovered, had been considered an exciting and innovative weapon by some when it was first manufactured in 1857, and was issued to cavalrymen during the Civil War. I now had a name, a time period, an occupation, and a location for the man whose life I was eventually to piece together from those first clues.

I continued to cull minor bits of information, picked up from one source or another, and to pursue each item until its place in Felsenthal's life was firmly fixed. This research procedure, of course, is analogous to solving a crossword puzzle: slowly separate items intersect and lead to yet new clues. But the intellectual challenge of asking the right questions of what little is available to draw out the maximum amount of new data is only part of the lure that keeps one researching. As the life I was investigating began to fill out, I found a curious thing happening. Louis Felsenthal came alive, not only to me, but also to my husband, whose enthusiasm and help on the project were unfailing. I am now aware that this is a common phenomenon among those who search out the lives of long-dead figures, but as it was happening I was amazed that Felsenthal had such a hold on our emotions. The day we learned where and when he had died, I was plunged into an irrational gloom. Intellectually I realized that surely he had died years earlier; however, emotionally I felt as though I had just received word of the death of a dear but distant friend.

I realized that my search was leading me to trace Felsenthal's life from birth to death, and so I began to conceive of the project as a biography. But I was troubled as I began to write because I had become fond of Felsenthal, and I had to come to grips with the need to present a balanced, objective account of someone I was obviously partial toward. I had been made aware of the importance of detachment and truth in life-writing by my friend and professor Lynn Z. Bloom, herself an accomplished biographer. In this account of Felsenthal's life, I have presented every major fact I uncovered, withholding nothing. I had none of his private papers or those of his peers which might give the personal account of motives from which to draw inferences about his character. Each reader must decide what impelled Felsenthal to do as he did in his life, but I believe him to have been an honest, forthright man firm in his convictions.

There is always the question of the value of chronicling the life of a man who had only a middling status. To that I answer that the field of biography is cluttered with those whose spectacular actions caused them to be famous or infamous. Why not give the history of a person who, like most of us, lived his life, did what circumstances and fate demanded of him, and contributed to his place and time, with little hope of being remembered in the future? Louis Felsenthal was, at the same time, both unique and Everyman. His life and actions were singularly representative of a colorful and important era in New Mexico history. I believe his story deserves to be known.

Finally I would like to express my gratitude to all those who so generously contributed their time and expertise to assisting me with this project, particularly Robert L. Meketa who helped with research in the Los Angeles area and Robert E. Fleming of the University of New Mexico who acted as advisor on the first draft.

Jacqueline Dorgan Meketa
Corrales, N.M.
November 1981

Louis Felsenthal
Citizen-Soldier of
Territorial New Mexico

"There is history in all men's lives."
Shakespeare,
Henry IV, Part 2, III.i.80.

1

Westward Voyager
1832–1858

The eight companies of infantrymen had left the fort early in the morning and marched northward on the west bank of the Rio Grande to a position from which they could protect the left and rear of the line of their Union comrades, who were fighting in the sand-hills on the east side of the river. A few hours later they were ordered southward once again, moving to stay positioned near the action. Finally, at one o'clock of the cold February afternoon in 1862, the order came from Regimental Commander Christopher (Kit) Carson, of the First New Mexico Volunteers, "Cross the river!"

Capt. Louis Felsenthal and the other company commanders led their men forward through the waist-deep waters, gained the other side, and pushed ahead four hundred yards into the chaos of smoke, gunfire, horses, and fighting men. At that moment, a body of five hundred of the Confederate enemy charged diagonally in front of the newly arrived infantrymen. As the head of the enemy column rushed to within eighty yards, Captain Felsenthal and his men, with the rest of Carson's Volunteers, fired a volley of deadly musket and revolver shots at the invading Texans. As they franti-

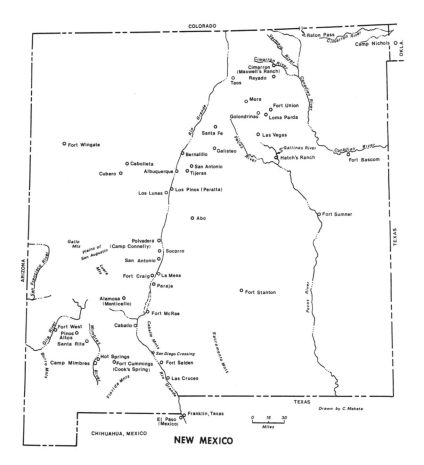

NEW MEXICO

4

cally reloaded and fired again, the boom of one of their own nearby cannons sounded and they saw a shell from the twenty-four pounder land, with deadly effect, in the midst of the enemy, who finally panicked, broke, and retreated in disorder.

Capt. Louis Felsenthal was only one of the many Union officers, both Regular Army and Volunteer, who fought at Valverde that day in the first major Civil War battle to take place in the Territory of New Mexico against the Confederates who had marched up the river from Texas. But in many ways he was very different from most of the other men commanding the troops. He was native to neither the Territory nor the Union he was defending, having arrived in America only a few years earlier. He had no prior military experience and, in fact, his background and training had prepared him for a much more sedentary and less dangerous kind of life.

Yet some of the officers on the battlefield that day did share Felsenthal's experience of having come to the Territory to seek opportunity. With the acquisition of the New Mexico Territory as a result of the 1846 Mexican-American War, a vast, almost untouched area of plains, deserts, and mountains had been opened up that attracted all who had the imagination, determination, and courage to challenge it. Many people today, influenced by history and folklore, tend to think of these pioneers as mental and physical giants. However, in reality, they were often just thousands of forgotten little people who did the humdrum jobs essential to each step taken to bring civilization to the West. They were merchants, farriers, miners, stablemen, clerks, minor public servants, hotelkeepers, infantrymen, telegraph operators, priests, and small farmers. Though their private lives were never recorded for posterity, all were important in their own way. Recording their lives provides a glimpse into the commonplace daily activities so necessary to sustain life in the area and permit the more exciting and historically significant events to take place—history from the bottom up in a sense.

Louis Felsenthal was such a man. A description of his life in the New Mexico Territory reveals much about the society, politics, and mores of his time. Felsenthal was a man of courage and intelligence who had a burning interest in history and a knowledge of its importance. He knew, worked with, fought with, and socialized with most of the men whose careers we know well from that tumultuous transitional period in New Mexico. Yet, somehow falling short of fame, Felsenthal has until now remained unknown and unmentioned. It is ironic that Felsenthal, exquisitely sensitive to the historical significance of the times he was living through, nearly failed to gain his minor place in the state's history.

Felsenthal arrived in Santa Fe only a few years after Gen. Stephen Watts Kearny's army invaded the area and proclaimed it a part of the United States. Life in the Territory at that time was hazardous, disorderly, antediluvian, and difficult, at least by today's standards. Nevertheless, during the second half of the nineteenth century, Felsenthal, like many other unsung and unremembered men, regarded the Territory as a genial home.

Louis Felsenthal was born in Iserlohn, Westphalia, Prussia, fifty miles northeast of Cologne in western Germany, on November 5, 1832.[1] He was the third child of a merchant, Jacob Abraham, and his wife, Hanne, who already had a five-year-old daughter, Rahle, and a three-year-old son, Gabriel. Seven years later they would complete their family with the arrival of a third son, Levi. Records show that from the middle of the eighteenth century, at least, the traditional family profession was that of Handelsmann, or merchant-dealer. At birth the child was given four names—Elieser, Jacob, Gotthelf, and Abraham—but no surname, as was the custom of Jewish families in Prussia at that time. However, in 1845, a law was passed requiring Jews to accept surnames, and the family took the name *Felsenthal,* which translated to Rock Valley and probably describes the physical characteristics of some nearby area that had personal significance to them. [2]

Political life was in flux in Prussia during the years of Felsenthal's youth. The people of the confederated states of Germany, tired of the rule of princes who wielded absolute power, were demanding a constitutional government: revolutionary turmoil was unleashed at various times, particularly in 1848. Under these troubled conditions, the Jews, who historically had been self-contained groups, probably tried to continue their daily lives in an inconspicuous manner. Since three generations of Felsenthal's family members had been leaders in the Jewish community of Iserlohn, there seems little doubt that he attended the Jewish ground (elementary) school and was raised in orthodox surroundings. Presumably, after completing his basic education, he attended private language schools in Iserlohn and gained there his proficiency in various languages.

After finishing school, Felsenthal took employment

as a clerk but at the age of twenty-one, in September 1854, he sought and was issued a passport for the stated purpose of allowing him to take a pleasure trip through the German Federal States and to Belgium. It would seem that the real purpose behind the application for the document was an impending emigration to the United States, for at that time he used the anglicized name Louis, a translation of the Eliesar he was given at birth. The passport described Felsenthal as only four feet eleven inches tall with dark-blond hair, eyebrows, and beard. It further stated that he had gray eyes, a face with oval chin and healthy complexion, an "ordinary" nose and mouth, and was of slight build.[3]

Presumably the money to pay for the trip to America was raised by Felsenthal's family because such a voyage across the Atlantic was expensive. It is not known what attributes or motives caused Felsenthal to be chosen over his older brother or whether he traveled from Belgium directly to the United States. But by 1858, Louis Felsenthal had already made his way across the ocean, most of the American continent, and was living in the City of the Holy Faith—Santa Fe.

At that time Santa Fe was a primitive town of adobe structures, dusty streets, Hispanic charm, and frontier gusto. Paradoxically, it was a young-old town. Only twelve years earlier the Americans and their army had marched into Santa Fe and captured it without a fight from the Mexicans who had controlled the territory for only twenty-five years after having declared their independence from Spain in 1821. The United States was in the process of trying to impose its efficient, materialistic life-style over the casual, slow-paced Latin ways that had been in effect since 1610 when Governor Pedro de Peralta, a Spanish explorer, founded the city on the site of some prehistoric Indian cultures. Situated at the terminus of the Santa Fe Trail, the city had, by the middle of the nineteenth century, developed into a "sin city" in some respects—a place where wagon-train travelers and soldiers could find a drink or a girl after weeks of deprivation.

Newcomers who visited Santa Fe around 1850 found it shockingly medieval when compared to the eastern United States.[4] They were unimpressed by flat-roofed homes and public buildings, even the Catholic parish church, which were constructed of mud bricks called adobes. They were dismayed at the crudely made, hand-hewn furniture and art objects; at the fact that bedsteads were mostly unknown and that the bedding was spread out on the dirt floors at night; and at the illiteracy of the people. The rules of social etiquette followed by these Spanish-speaking Catholics were so alien to the Anglo-Americans that they sometimes brought a blush to the cheeks of so-called proper visiting eastern ladies, although the men often seemed to find them charming. The señoritas of New Mexico wore much more comfortable and revealing clothing than their eastern sisters, and often went barefooted around the house. They freely and openly smoked cigarillos and one of their main diversions was dancing, both at the fandangos or public dances, and at the bailes, which were more formal. Another favorite pastime was wagering; during the early years of the American occupation, New Mexican women of all classes were regular visitors to the many gambling houses in operation about the city. This custom later died out, evidently a victim of American disapproval. The local ladies, less repressed by social conventions than eastern women, were considered gay, friendly, and quite beautiful by the Anglo men who admired their jet-black eyes and slender, delicate frames.

It is to be wondered at, then, how this young Prussian Jew, Louis Felsenthal, came to settle in this exotic yet backward area where little more than the absolute necessities to sustain life were available due to the lack of local industries and the expense of manufactured goods brought in over the perilous plains from the East. What circumstances brought him to this town, so opposite in every way from the refined old-world atmosphere of his German homeland where centuries of European culture had developed an orderly and mannered civilization? A definitive answer cannot be given, for the details are unknown, but some educated guessing is possible.

Coinciding with the economic and political chaos in central Europe from the late 1830s through the 1850s was the rapid growth and expansion of the young country, America, across the ocean. Word of this democracy's equality for all citizens and unlimited possibilities for individual success had been making its way across the Atlantic, so it is no wonder that, after the European depression of 1836, and during the revolutionary upheavals in Prussia during the late 1840s and early 1850s, many German Jews emigrated to the United States. Some, unfamiliar with this country, settled first in New York City where they had disembarked from their ships. Most were involved in commerce or banking, the fields in which they already had expertise. A large percentage were single men who hoped to work themselves into more favorable circumstances in the United States where opportunities were believed to be open for those willing to work hard and employ good judgment. Often several young male relatives emigrated together, and sometimes, after a business had been established and was prospering, other members of the family or close friends were sent money for passage to America. These Jewish men kept a close eye on the commercial conditions in the country and were always alert for new markets.

In 1846, when Kearny's army made its bloodless invasion of the Mexican government's northern province of New Mexico and took possession of it, the main motivation had not been military but rather economic—a desire to avoid disturbing the profitable Santa Fe trade. The Jewish merchants were sage enough to realize that, with the acquisition of the area, trade with the entire West was being opened up. It is not strange, then, that observers in New Mexico quickly noted a rapidly increasing population of Jewish origin, principally from New York.

These pioneers were not impractical dreamers but hardheaded businessmen who were aware that sacrifices were a part of the gamble to make their fortune. They were prepared to wager what assets they already had; to endure physical discomfort, danger, and separation from friends and family; to learn the new ways and new languages necessary to conduct their businesses; to face possible rejection in an alien society; and above all to work the long hours necessary for success. Surely Louis Felsenthal considered and accepted these conditions when he decided to chance his future in the Southwest.

11

2

The Adobe Capital
1858–1860

In 1858, in order to reach Santa Fe from the East, Louis Felsenthal first had to journey to the Missouri-Kansas border where parties headed west assembled. Regardless of the mode of travel he chose, he would most probably have started out from Independence, Missouri, the main eastern terminal of the Santa Fe Trail. The fastest method of passage would have been by one of the stage coaches, drawn by six mules, which carried the United States mail across the plains, with departures scheduled for the first and fifteenth of each month. Although an occasional trip was recorded in the exceptional time of slightly under twenty days, the average travel time by stage was between twenty-five and thirty days, barring, of course, unforseen problems such as Indian attacks and severe equipment breakdowns. The traveler was charged one hundred fifty dollars for his fare during the winter months but there was a twenty-five dollar reduction for those who preferred a summer trip. In addition, the passenger was charged thirty-five to fifty cents a pound, depending again on the season, for transportation of his baggage, which was limited to forty pounds, exclusive of his bedding.[1]

For this price, those making the journey could expect to be packed tightly into a coach that had been designed for fewer people, to endure thirst in the summer and extreme cold in the winter, to suffer bone-jolting extended runs with infrequent stops, and on occasions to find themselves in the company of drunken and often profane companions who found liquor the most effective anesthesia against the interminable monotony of the prairie landscape and the exhausting tension brought on by fear of Indian attack. Male passengers were expected to assist with any problems the stage encountered, whether it be a malfunction, miring in deep mud or snow, an overturned coach, or the surprise appearance of hostile Comanches, Kiowas, or other Plains Indians. To this end, the proprietors of the line supplied each male passenger with arms and ammunition.[2]

There were both advantages and disadvantages to choosing the alternative mode of travel—the wagon train. The trip from Kansas to Santa Fe could take twice as long and the slow-moving wagons made the trains more vulnerable targets than the faster stagecoaches. However, the additional men in a wagon-train party ensured more firepower in the event of an attack and provided companionship. The large wagons also offered more comfortable accommodations, allowed for transportation of more personal luggage, and enabled the passengers an opportunity to stretch their legs by walking alongside the moving caravan.

Regardless of the type of transportation he chose, Louis Felsenthal slept each night on the ground, exposed to the elements and serenaded by the yelps and calls of coyotes and wolves. He ate spartan meals cooked over an open campfire, worried about the two deadly scourges of those who were crossing the plains—cholera and Indian marauders—and undoubtedly was awed by great herds of bison and antelope that still abounded on the great prairies. From Independence to Santa Fe, more than 800 miles lay ahead to test the traveler's mettle.

After what must have seemed an almost endless trek, Louis Felsenthal undoubtedly would have been filled with curiosity and anticipation about Santa Fe. As the travelers crested the last small hill and gained their first sight of the town that had long been their goal, Felsenthal may well have been disappointed, for others have described their dismay, saying the place looked like nothing more than a brickyard of stacked adobes.[3]

Once they entered Santa Fe, the wagon trains traditionally made their way to the plaza in the center of town where they unloaded passengers and freight. As Felsenthal climbed down from the vehicle which had brought him so far, he surely looked about him with interest. Instead of green, fenced lawns he would have seen the simple houses surrounded by hard-packed dirt yards in which there might be a haystack, some chickens, or an outdoor mud-brick oven for breadbaking. He may have seen one of the local wood sellers, leading his tiny burro, laden with piñon wood from the nearby mountains, the essential fuel for both heating and cooking. The streets were unpaved, dusty in summer, muddy when the winter snows melted, and rutted with cart tracks the rest of the time. And surrounding the newly arrived stagecoach would have been a crowd of swarthy-skinned, exotically dressed natives, chattering excitedly in Spanish, for the arrival of a coach from the East was an event of major importance and interest to those so cut off from the rest of the world. Although a hotel, the Exchange, had been taken over by Anglos shortly after the arrival of the American conquerors, Felsenthal would have found it to be a single-storied structure of the pervasive adobe, hardly what he would have been accustomed to in hostelries. Even as he began to search for lodgings Felsenthal must have been dismayed for most houses were built with a crude, unprotected doorway adjacent to the street, earth floors, and a roof of dirt and tree boughs supported by rafters of rough tree trunks called vigas. But overshadowing the humble aura and the discomforts of the town was the natural beauty of its setting. With their homes situated a mile above sea level, Santa Fe's residents breathed a crystalline, invigorating mountain air, basked in sunshine almost every day of the year, and enjoyed the sight of cerulean skies and the evergreen-covered "Blood of Christ" mountains.

As much of a surprise as Santa Fe may have been, however, it seems probable that Felsenthal had at least cursory information about the place before he arrived, for his decision to travel to the trans-American West seemed hardly impulsive. It is probable that Felsenthal's trip had been carefully planned; that he had a definite destination and contacts awaiting him in Santa Fe. In 1856, a year and a half after Felsenthal had been issued his passport in Prussia, the firm of Seligman Brothers, Santa Fe traders, was founded under the name of Seligman & Clever. The names of Bernard Seligman and Charles Clever[4] appear repeatedly on documents and papers referring to Felsenthal over the next forty-four years and at one period in his life, Louis Felsenthal worked as a claims agent in Clever's law office. The Seligman family, like Felsenthal's grandfather, father, and younger brother, Levi, had been merchants in Prussia, and Charles Clever's home had been Cologne, only fifty miles from Iserlohn. Even if there was no family relationship between Felsenthal and one of the two Santa Fe traders, it seems probable that there had been a friendship or communication between them even before Felsenthal left Europe. Less than two years after the Santa Fe business had been set up, Felsenthal was on the scene and involved in social activities with the two men.

There is nothing surprising about the fact that Felsenthal showed up in Santa Fe rather than another town in New Mexico, for Santa Fe *was*, in essence, New Mexico. There were smaller villages located in places such as Taos, Albuquerque, Socorro, and Las Vegas, but it was in Santa Fe that the United States had set up a territorial government in 1851 with a governor, district judges who sat together as the supreme court, and a legislative assembly of two chambers. Santa Fe was the hub of the New Mexico Territory, which encompassed an enormous area of wilderness and desert that also included the land which is now the state of Arizona and the portion of Colorado which lies south of the Arkansas River. The city was the commercial, legislative, judicial, and military center of power. It was a crossroad, the northern end of the Chihuahua Trail, which shuttled goods into the interior of northern Mexico, as well as the western conclusion of the Santa Fe Trail, the funnel through which goods, news, and federal instructions flowed from the East. It was the central point from which orders were issued to the outlying military forts established in an attempt to safeguard travelers and settlers from the terrorizing raids of the hostile Indians who still had the power to attack, burn, kill, and steal livestock or hostages. Two-thirds of the German-Jewish population of New Mexico, who were mainly merchants and bankers, was concentrated in Santa Fe before 1860.[5]

Felsenthal seems to have settled into life in Santa Fe quickly. By December 1859, a little more than a year after he had arrived in the city, he acquired the position of clerk of the House for the Ninth Territorial Legislative Assembly convening there. Possibly he got the job because of his education, previous clerical experience in Europe, or his facility with languages, since interpreters were an essential part of New Mexico's legislature. Most members of the assembly were of Hispanic background, were new to United States citizenship, and spoke not a word of English. While they were enthusiastic and anxious to please, most were unfamiliar with American governmental procedures. Documents and oral proceedings had to be translated into both Spanish and English for clarity.

It was also surely to Felsenthal's advantage that he already knew many of the most important people in Santa Fe. Only two years earlier his friend Charles Clever had served as clerk of the Territorial Council, and perhaps he had used his influence to help Felsenthal obtain his position. But, regardless of how he got the job, Felsenthal found himself a part of the controversy surrounding the New Mexico version of the slave debate, which was then rampant across the United States and a preamble to the Civil War.

Throughout the country, at that time, southern sympathizers and northern antislave factions were attempting to consolidate strength in the various states and territories and New Mexico was no exception. Due to the influence of Miguel Otero, the New Mexico territorial delegate in Washington and a man partial to the southern cause, the local legislature passed a slave code in 1859. The code, similar to the National Fugitive Slave Act, applied only to slaves of African origins. The irony was that although there were only a handful of Negro slaves in the Territory, mostly belonging to Regular Army officers, the practice of peonage of both Hispanos and captured Apache and Navajo Indians was widespread in New Mexico. It had been in effect since the seventeenth century and the peons, controlled under the system by indebtedness, were treated much less humanely than Negro slaves in the South. The wealthy men, to whom they were indebted, had no obligation to care for them when they became too old to work. In addition, even though, in theory, the peons were not to be bought or sold, in practice they were reportedly often as much an article of trade as a horse or a sheep.

Not all the local legislators, however, approved of the slave code and during the Ninth Legislative Session while Felsenthal was serving as clerk of the House, the house speaker, Levi Keithly, unexpectedly introduced a repeal measure to the slave code. Reportedly, Keithly was a plain, honest, straightforward old farmer, a man inexperienced in political maneuvering, and he naively expected that his repeal bill would pass on its own merits. According to a report of the incident, when "those corrupt office-holders who had procured the passage of the law" heard of the repeal bill, they immediately planned a strategy to prevent it from coming before the House for discussion. "That night," the report continues, "government officials kept open house. John Barleycorn did his work, and 'mint drops' were freely administered where other means failed."[6] The report further states that a "Mexican" (the term used at that time to denote those local people whose mother tongue was Spanish) was promised Keithly's position as speaker if he would employ his influence to defeat the bill. Evidently the report was correct, if possibly somewhat biased, for *The New Mexico Blue Book of 1882*, an official legislative publication, shows that Mr. Keithly was replaced by a Celso C. Medina as House Speaker in 1859, and the slave code remained in effect, much to the disgust of the famous New York *Tribune* editor, Horace Greeley. Greeley wrote, "A Slave Code of signal atrocity and inhumanity has been put through the Territorial Legislature, and is now in full force."[7] Greeley was so incensed by what he felt was the growing proslavery sentiment in New Mexico that he reserved his most castigating criticism for the natives, and wrote:

The mass of the people are Mexicans—a hybrid race of Spanish and Indian origin. They are ignorant and degraded, demoralized and priest-ridden. The debasing Mexican system of peonage—a modified slavery—is still maintained there. A few able and unscrupulous men control everything. The masses are their blind, facile tools. There is no Press of any account; no Public Opinion; of course, no Republican party. Slavery rules all.[8]

In his position as clerk of the House, Felsenthal surely heard the rumors that flew about the halls of the legislature and was able to observe at close hand the political maneuverings of the men of power in the new Territory. It is impossible to know where his sentiments lay on the slavery issue, but as a member of a historically isolated and persecuted religious group, it seems probable that Felsenthal leaned toward the northern cause. In less than a year and a half he was to be faced with the decision of whether or not to back his sentiments with practical action.

In the meantime, however, Felsenthal was widening his circle of acquaintances among the influential men of the city. Evidence of this activity was an event that took place on the day after Christmas in 1859 when a group of prominent citizens met to charter a new social and cultural organization and Felsenthal was among them. Obviously feeling that Santa Fe was overendowed with bars and dance halls but sadly lacking in educational, historical, and quasi-scientific information and displays, the gentlemen banded together to organize the first Historical Society of New Mexico. They drew up and approved a constitution and the signatures surrounding Felsenthal's attest to the excellent company he was keeping, for the most important men in Santa Fe at that time became members. They included the following: Abraham Rencher, governor of the Territory; the famed Bishop Lamy; Kirby Benedict, then chief justice of the Supreme Court of the Territory; Joab Houghton, who, as a territorial judge had presided over the treason trials at Taos after the murder of the first American governor, Charles Bent, in 1847; Zadoc Staab and Bernard Seligman, two German-Jewish merchants of considerable prestige in both financial and political circles; Charles Clever; and various other Santa Feans of high repute. The Society was quite selective and set up a system by which it could reject any applicants the members might feel were morally or socially unacceptable. For admittance a man had to submit two letters of recommendation and receive a 75 percent vote of approval from the entire membership. In just two short months, the committees formed by enthusiastic Society members had designed a seal and sent the pattern to New York to be engraved and had sent a bilingual set of Society by-laws off to St. Louis for publication. In addition, they had outfitted and furnished, even to window curtains, a hall they were renting from Bishop Lamy for twelve dollars a month to house the new organization.[9] Members generously donated items to help build the fledgling Society's collection, and the gifts ranged from the practical—books, maps, and money—to the exotic—the bead-ornamented ear of an Arapahoe Indian, an ambrotype of a famous Mexican dwarf, a sea horse, and an Indian birch bark canoe from Canada. The March 1860 donation list quizzically mentions, "From Mr. L. Felsenthal, one rare skin of an unknown animal."[10] In April, members were assigned to "Sections" covering the various areas of interest to the Society. Felsenthal was appointed to serve on the Geology and Mineralogy Section along with a merchant, an army officer, a Protestant minister, a physician, and several other men.[11]

The Society continued to grow and hold its monthly meetings through 1860 and into 1861. Individuals often presented papers or reports on subjects as diversified as geography and Indian history. In 1861, after having been a member for a year and a half, Louis Felsenthal made two unique and interesting donations. He gave the Society, on two separate occasions, in May and June, the epaulettes and antique Spanish dragoon pistol of a Mexican Army officer who had become a hero, twenty-four years earlier, by almost single-handedly putting down an Indian revolt at Santa Cruz de la Cañada in northern New Mexico, in 1837.[12] This officer, Capt. Pedro Muñoz of the Vera Cruz dragoons, had rushed upon the insurgents and killed their leader when Gen. Manuel Armijo, a former governor of the Mexican Territory and leader of the counterrevolutionary army, had faltered and fearfully begun to fall back without venturing an attack. It is interesting to speculate about where Felsenthal acquired these items, for Captain Muñoz was already dead at the time Felsenthal made the donation. But they do point out Felsenthal's interest in history and his awareness of the importance of preserving pertinent items. Throughout his life he continued to acquire and save records and physical mementoes of historical importance, many of a military nature, and sometimes even placed himself in some jeopardy to do so.

But his interest in history was not the only factor that helped Louis Felsenthal make friends and begin to feel at home in his adopted land. In addition there was his religion. He was one of the small group of Jews who celebrated the first High Holy Days in New Mexico when they met together for Yom Kippur in 1860. Santa Fe had no temple and that year, at the invitation of Mrs. Levi Spiegelberg, a seventeen-year-old who had been married only a few months earlier and come to the West, the group assembled in the parlors of the only two-story house in the city, hers. Of the eighteen people present, only two were women, the hostess and her sister-in-law, Mrs. Sol Spiegelberg. A report of the gathering printed many years later in *The American Israelite* in Cincinnati, Ohio, on February 13, 1881, said,

How we remained together all that long day until night fasting, praying, and seeing who could fast the best. It was a strange crowd in that Catholic country, where Indian fights, murders, broils and fandangos were everyday occurrences; but that motley crowd consisted of men and women whose hearts beat for Israel. . . . Finally, the ladies had prepared for us a grand feast, and we were in just such condition to do it justice, and after a pleasant evening's chat ended the first Yom Kippur held in Santa Fe . . . "

In his letters home to Iserlohn, Felsenthal could report with satisfaction that things were going well. He was becoming accepted and important in Santa Fe's non-Hispanic society with opportunities for a future in politics or business open to him. But life in Santa Fe, as in the rest of the United States, was about to be disrupted by the Civil War, and neither Santa Fe nor Felsenthal would be the same when it ended.

3

Civil War Soldier
1861–1862

During 1859 and 1860, while intrigues were hatched, charges and countercharges hurled by proponents of both the northern and southern causes, and threats and political tricks employed by both sides, it appeared to many observers that New Mexico would ally itself with the Confederates. But with the secession of the southern states from the Union in the spring of 1861, most of the ranking army officials in the Territory resigned their commissions and left New Mexico to offer their services to the Confederacy. Much of the prosouthern strength left with them. The Regular Army detachments, which had been charged with suppressing the hostile Indians, were sorely weakened by the southerners' departure. Additional federal troops were soon siphoned off from the territorial army detachments to bolster Union troops in the East.

Because of their diminished numbers, the Regular Army soldiers in New Mexico were withdrawn from the outlying forts and consolidated in a few key posts. The Apaches and Navajos immediately took advantage of the situation, especially in western New Mexico, and began a reign of terror, attacking villages, capturing numerous women and children, and causing many inhabitants to abandon their homes and hurry to fortified places. To add to this turmoil, the less respectable elements of the local populace seized the opportunity to show general disregard for the law. As a result of the chaotic conditions that prevailed throughout New Mexico during the summer of 1861, the peaceful inhabitants lost faith in the ability of the federal military forces to protect them.

Col. Edward R. S. Canby, recently appointed commandant of the Ninth Military District, had received intelligence reports that Confederate forces from Texas might invade New Mexico in an attempt to sever the Southwest from the Union and secure the gold fields of California and Colorado for the South. He knew his limited federal troops would be totally inadequate to repel the Texans, and he endeavored to raise a volunteer force among the local populace. But the natives remained generally apathetic. They were too much distracted by serious internal problems. After all, the gringo soldiers were not even able to keep the marauding Indians and the other lawbreakers under control and besides, the Spanish-speaking peons had little knowledge of or interest in preserving some government based far away in Washington. Another factor that influenced some of the local people was the rumor, circulated by southern sympathizers, that if the natives joined the Union forces, a Texan army, then on the borders of New Mexico, would supply the Indians with arms to attack them. The attitude of many New Mexicans was succinctly expressed in a *Santa Fe Gazette* editorial of May 11, 1861, which began, "What is the position of New Mexico? The answer is a short one. She desires to be let alone."

If the general population was totally apathetic, the same could not be said of many prominent men in Santa Fe. They were well aware of the possible disastrous consequences of an invasion by Confederate troops. As early as May 1861, then-Governor Henry Connelly and Colonel Canby requested the assistance of some of the Territory's best-known citizens and they began making and implementing plans for the establishment of a volunteer force to help defend New Mexico. One of the incentives offered was the promise of officer commissions to those who could recruit enough men to raise a company.

Louis Felsenthal could hardly have forseen that, less than three years after his arrival in Santa Fe, he would have found himself in a situation such as this. Only the year before he had received the distressing news that his father had died in Iserlohn and the decision had been made for his mother to live with Levi, now twenty-one.[1] His personal assets, as he had declared to the 1860 census taker, amounted to only five hundred dollars, and he was working as a clerk. Now Santa Fe was in an uproar; rumors flew, meetings were held, decisions made.

Finally, in late July 1861, the dreaded word came. The Texans, under Col. John R. Baylor, had invaded near El Paso and marched north to Mesilla, about two hundred and eighty miles to the south of Santa Fe. They occupied the town, which had a large prosouthern faction among its citizenry, without difficulty. Baylor then prepared to attack Fort Fillmore, six miles to the southeast, even though he knew that the Union troops there outnumbered his force by about three hundred men. On July 27, 1861, as Baylor's troops approached,

Union Army Maj. Isaac Lynde hastily abandoned the post, ordering his men to march to Fort Stanton, one hundred and fifty miles away. Baylor's Texans had little problem in overtaking and capturing many of the Union soldiers who were suffering from thirst in their precipitous and ill-conceived flight across the desert. This was the first Union defeat of the Civil War in New Mexico, and the Confederates would surely march north. The news electrified the more educated and sophisticated population of Santa Fe, both Anglo and native, and they accelerated their defense plans.

Louis Felsenthal apparently had decided, a month or more before the actual invasion, to volunteer to serve the Union and had begun recruiting men for a company of infantrymen to be part of the First Regiment of New Mexico Volunteers. The job would not be an easy one because much competition existed among the various potential company commanders, with each trying to fill his ranks with able-bodied men from among a citizenry not particularly enthusiastic about volunteering. Felsenthal enlisted the aid of Pantaleon Archuleta with the promise that he could become first lieutenant of the incipient company if they were successful in forming it. While Felsenthal used his powers of persuasion in Santa Fe, Archuleta set to work signing up men in Rio Arriba county, his home territory. By July 20, approximately forty men, or half a company's strength, had been recruited. Archuleta was then given his commission at Plaza Alcalde near Española. Four days later, in Santa Fe, Antonio Abeytia was sworn in as second lieutenant and on July 30, even though the company was still less than 75 percent filled, Felsenthal was permitted to sign the Muster-In-

Rolls to be commissioned a captain and commander of Company "G".

It is interesting to speculate about Felsenthal's motivation for abandoning his work and civilian life to rush forward to volunteer to serve in the defense of the Territory. He had no prior military experience; he had not traveled widely throughout the rough areas outside of Santa Fe; he had been living the sedentary life of a clerk with its ledgers and paperwork and dabbling in some minor merchandising on the side. Now he was offering to recruit a company of men and lead them into battle. Perhaps the excitement of the stirred-up population infected him or possibly he had always harbored a secret longing for the military life and visualized himself as a leader of men. He would soon be twenty-nine years old and may have felt this would be his last opportunity to fill a glamorous role. He also could have experienced a strong patriotic fervor to defend his newly found homeland or may have been influenced by friends who were also joining. Whatever his reasons, Felsenthal now had a difficult task ahead of him.

Two of the most famous men in New Mexico headed the First Regiment, New Mexico Volunteers. Col. Christopher "Kit" Carson, nationally famous as an Indian fighter and skilled mountain man, was commanding officer.[2] Second-in-command was Lt. Col. J. Francisco Chaves, a prominent native, the son of a former governor under the Mexican rule and the stepson of Governor Henry Connelly, who was in office at the time. Felsenthal was one of ten captains commanding the companies of the regiment and must have felt it a singular honor to serve under the famed "Kit"

Carson, who, like Felsenthal, was also a man of small physical stature.

The need for a strong volunteer force was desperate because the number of federal troops in the Territory was ludicrously insufficient to face the many soldiers the Confederate invasion army was expected to contain. Washington would not spare Union troops from farther east, and even though a plea for help had gone out to Colorado and California, should they have responded with aid, it might come too late.

The situation was critical. Although the first regiment of infantrymen had been partially staffed and was in the process of being trained, more soldiers were desperately needed and recruiting was not going well, as Felsenthal had discovered. Colonel Canby and Governor Connelly realized that immediate action must be taken now that the Texans were on New Mexico soil, and they knew that it was futile to appeal to the natives with a plea to preserve the Union.

Connelly, whose years of living in New Mexico had given him a thorough understanding of the Mexican temperament, knew that the natives had a long-standing fear of and hatred for Texans. Twenty years before, Texas had sent an expedition north to try to capture Santa Fe from the Mexican government then in power. The Texans had been taken prisoner by local Mexican troops about forty miles southeast of the city near San Miguel del Vado. They had been forced on a deadly march, under guard, all the way down to Mexico City. Many of the Texans had been mistreated and died on the long march, and rumor now had it that they would be vengeful upon their return. Many of the natives feared that the Texans' pride and bitterness over the old defeat would make them keen to retaliate for past wrongs. This was the weapon Governor Connelly used, issuing proclamations in Spanish and English urging the natives to arms, saying of the Texans, "Their long smothered vengeance against our Territory and people, they now seek to gratify," and telling them, "You cannot, you must not, hesitate to take up arms in defense of your homes, firesides, and families."[3]

Felsenthal's fluency in Spanish was probably a great advantage in his recruiting endeavors, and it was the Spanish-speaking populace that eventually contributed almost all of the enlisted men in the Volunteers.

Less than two weeks after it had become an official entity, Felsenthal's Company "G" was organized and outfitted enough at Fort Marcy to be sent on its first assignment, duty at Fort Union.[4]

This must have been a hectic time for the little captain because he would have had to put all his personal affairs in order and have a uniform of Federal blue tailored. It was probably at this time that he purchased his Maynard carbine and had the silver plaque inserted in the stock on which he ordered engraved his name, rank, and regimental designation.[5]

Felsenthal's company was one of the earliest to be organized and go on active duty. Colonel Canby had expressed a desire for a total of thirty-two companies of volunteers, and long after Felsenthal and his men were in the field, recruiting efforts continued unabated. Although the New Mexicans started from a position of incredible military weakness, through the efforts of Governor Connelly, Colonel Canby, and many forgotten men like Louis Felsenthal, what had appeared at first to be an impossible task was accomplished.

Eventually between three and four thousand volunteers had signed up, arms had been issued to them, and some measure of fighting spirit had been aroused. The fear in Santa Fe had been that the Texans would quickly follow up on their initial victory and begin marching north toward the city. However, this did not happen and throughout the late summer and fall, the New Mexico Volunteers gained time to organize, outfit themselves, and acquire some rudimentary training. This temporary reprieve came about because the original invading force was only 258 Texas cavalrymen. While they had been highly successful and had captured two forts in the south near the Mexican border, they obviously were insufficient in number to continue the campaign. The Confederates had planned to follow their original attack quickly with an invading army, but conditions forced them to divert it to eastern service. To secure another force to attack New Mexico, the Confederates granted Col. Henry H. Sibley an independent command and authorization to raise an army in Texas. Until the end of 1861, Sibley was busy recruiting and outfitting his 3,700-man army and during the same time the federal troops and volunteers in New Mexico were preparing their defenses.

In mid-August, when Captain Felsenthal and his newly organized company reached Fort Union, they were assigned to assist in the construction of a new Star Fort being hurriedly raised there with the aim of increasing the defensive capability of the post. Fort Union was vital to the protection of the western part of the Santa Fe Trail, over which all military supplies were arriving. It was also expected to be crucial in stopping any Confederate advance from the south or southeast. To get to Fort Union the new recruits and their novice commander, being infantrymen, had walked. The 110-mile march, which took about a week, was their introduction into the life of the soldier. It can well be imagined that there were second thoughts among some of the footweary men by the time Fort Union came into view. Then, in short order, they were issued shovels and axes and put to work constructing the massive earthen field work. They were beginning to learn, as centuries of soldiers before them had, that military service is more often arduous and filled with drudgery than spangled with glory.

The Rio Grande, though unnavigable, has been, since the time of aboriginal tribes, the highway through New Mexico. It runs almost through the center of the state, from its northernmost boundary all the way south. In a vast, dry, trackless expanse of desert, it has been both a guiding feature and a source of water. Colonel Canby, the Union commander, knew that if the Confederates invaded from the south they would come up the river since most of the settlements in the Territory were situated along its banks and thus foraging would be easier for the invaders. Colonel Canby also knew that he had a limited number of troops so he abandoned all of the major forts in the Territory except two. He concentrated his men at Fort Craig on the Rio Grande, 30 miles south of Socorro, to protect the southern third of the Territory and at Fort Union, 100 miles northeast of Santa Fe, near the junction of the Mountain and Cimarron Branches of the Santa Fe Trail, as insurance against a possible move from the east by the Confederates.

Southwest corner of the Plaza in Santa Fe c. 1855, a few years before Louis Felsenthal arrived in the Territory. The Exchange Hotel is in the center and Seligman and Clever's store at the right. (Courtesy Museum of New Mexico, Photo Collections)

L. J. Keithly, speaker of the House during the Ninth Legislative Session of the Territorial Legislative Assembly in Santa Fe in 1859. Felsenthal served as a clerk to the House during this session. (Courtesy Museum of New Mexico, Photo Collections)

Tintype of Union Army officers in Santa Fe, c. 1862.
Felsenthal is seated at the far right, but the others in the
photograph are unidentified. (Courtesy Museum of New
Mexico, Photo Collections)

Facing Page: The reroofed Jesus Abreu house at Rayado, New
Mexico where Felsenthal and his company of infantrymen found
refuge during a severe and prolonged snowstorm in 1864.
(Photograph by Charles E. Meketa)

Above, left: Jesus G. Abreu, a native New Mexican, was the brother of Col. Francisco Abreu, second-in-command of Felsenthal's infantry regiment. (Courtesy of the Philmont Scout Ranch)

Above, right: Maj. Arthur Morrison, stationed at Fort Craig in the winter of 1861 with Felsenthal, commanded the small contingent of advance troops that manned the post until Colonel Carson arrived in January 1862. (Courtesy Museum of New Mexico, Photo Collections)

Gray's Ranch C.T.
October 20th 1864.

Sir,

I have the honor herewith to enclose a letter just received from the Commanding Officer at Ft Lyon C.T. which will give information of the position I occupy here. I also enclose Special Order No. 223 issued at said post which shows, that regardless to the Orders I give to the Non-Commissioned Officers of detachments, I send to Fort Lyon as escorts to the U.S. Mail, generally said detachments are retained at Ft Lyon, and treated as a Company there. — Most of the transportation, for which I am responsible is now at Ft Lyon, and I do not know, what has or will became of the same. —

My provisions is nearly out and if matters go on this way, my Company will soon be at Ft Lyon and I with my first Sergeant and buglers, will be left alone to guard the Camp and escort the mails. —

The mails which arrive here pretend that there is no danger at all on the road between Ft Lyon and Ft Union, and do not travel with or avail themselves of the escort. —

I am encamped here on the River, without any other shelter, than a few brush-huts, the days, and especially the nights are very cold, and we have snow-storms here every few days, in consequence of which the men (they having but little clothing) are suffering very much. —

The mules I took with me from Ft Union are nearly exhausted and several of them, had also to be left on the

roads, being unable to proceed any further, two of them
have died; two more trips will leave me without
any animals. —

I state all these facts in order to get from the
Commanding Officer at Fort Union the necessary directions
in regard to what I shall & do. —

The sixty days, for which I was detailed,
being out on the last of this month and my
provisions also, I shall proceed to Fort Union
on the 26th inst; with what men and transportation I have here, unless I receive an order
to the Contrary. —

I have the honor to remain Sir

Very Respectfully
Your Obedient Servant

To the Post Adjutant
Fort Union N. M.

Capt 1st Infty N.M. Vols
Com'dg Co "C"

A letter from Felsenthal to the post adjutant, Fort Union, on
October 20, 1864. Felsenthal, then at Gray's Ranch, protested
that his soldiers were being detained at Fort Lyon. (Courtesy
The National Archives)

Rayado N. M.
November 9th 1864

Sir,

I have the honor to submit the following for the consideration of the Commanding Officer.—

I left Gray's Ranch C.T. with my Company on the 29th of October last. On arriving at the foot of the Summit of the Raton Pass, we were caught in a severe Snow Storm.— Under great difficulties we got to Red River Station that day.— It snowed all that night, and next morning, the Snow on the level ground measured 19 Inches deep, Snowing still, and continuing so all day long. I remained at Red River Station for two days, but there being no forage, nor shelter for either men or beasts, I concluded to march on, to some place, where I might obtain both.— It took us four days & very hard labor to come from Red River Station to Mr Maxwell's Ranch and not being able to obtain there, what we needed, we proceeded to Rayado where we arrived two days ago.— For miles and miles the Company had to march through Snow which reached to their waist-belts, and had even then to assist in pulling, and pushing the Wagons.— I was fortunate enough to lose no mules, but they are utterly exhausted and need good rest and care, before I will be able to proceed. Many of my men had parts of their feet frozen, and the majority got Snowblind.

Having no Provisions, Mr Jesus Abreu here has been kind enough to furnish to my Company, what provisions they needed under the condition to return the same

A letter from Felsenthal to the post adjutant, Fort Union, on November 9, 1864. The winter march and the privations suffered by his men and their animals are recounted. (Courtesy The National Archives)

Bayard Cr. N.M.
Novbr. 14th 1864

Sir!

I have the honor to acknowledge the Receipt of your letter of the 13th inst, which was delivered to me at 3 Oclock P.M. this day, by Corpl. Quintana of my Company. The rations referred to, in the same, I received last Saturday; they will last my Command, with the provisions I obtained from Mr Jesus Abreu here, for eight days. The cause why I was, and am delayed here, I have fully explained to you in my letter dated Nov. 9th and which I forwarded by a Mr. W. Jones from Denver, who was going to Fort Union with a drove of beef-cattle, destined for Fort Union. I hope that by this time said letter has been delivered to you. The same causes I gave you as a reason for my remaining here, are still in existence, most of my Mules being yet utterly unable to stand the trip from here to Fort Union.

By the same Mr Jones, I sent a letter to the A.Q.M., Major Enos, suggesting to him to send me fresh Mules and leave the ones I have here with Mr. Abreu, who has got good Stables and plenty of good forage for them. The same suggestion I would herewith renew, for the reason, that I sincerely believe to loose every Mule I have with me, if I should undertake a trip with them now, in their present state of exhaustion and on a road in a condition to kill fresh and healthy animals. If on the other hand the necessary rest and care is allowed them, they will assuredly be saved for the Government.

Whilst writing this I receive notice, that of those men, detained at Fort Lyon, 16 had arrived 8 miles from here, and they will be here to morrow. They have got 2 wagons and 8 mules with them. They are in a deplorable condition.

I am forced to remain here until the roads get a little more practicable or until I receive fresh animals; I would not willingly remain here one hour longer than I can help it, but the circumstances, which constrain me, are somewhat beyond my control.

Hoping to be more fortunate this time in soliciting an answer and some instructions, having received no answer to any of my previous letters and requests for instructions, I have the honor to remain

With the greatest respect
Your Obt. Sot.
Louis Felsenthal
Capt. 1 Inf. N.M.V.
Commdg Comp. C

To Lt. John Lewis
Post Adjt.
Fort Union, Fort Union N.M.

Letter from Felsenthal to Lt. John Lewis, post adjutant, Fort Union on November 14, 1864. Supplies from the post had arrived, but the mules were not ready for a march. (Courtesy The National Archives)

A portrait of military officers stationed in Santa Fe taken c. 1866. Felsenthal is seated in the center, with Capt. Cyrus deForest, Gen. James H. Carleton's aide, seated to the right. Standing to the right is Brevet Col. David Huntington, U.S. Army surgeon. The other men are unidentified. (Courtesy Museum of New Mexico, Photo Collections)

Group of Santa Fe citizens, c. 1867. Felsenthal is third from the left, standing; seated at the far right is Dr. J. Cooper McKee, prominent Civil War surgeon in the Union Army; all the other men are unidentified. (Courtesy Museum of New Mexico, Photo Collections, photograph by Nicholas Brown)

Fort Union, New Mexico, during the Civil War. Felsenthal
was stationed there several times during the War, and it was
his headquarters when dispatched to guard the Santa Fe Trail.
(Courtesy Museum of New Mexico, Photo Collections,
photograph by the U.S. Army Signal Corps)

Lucien Maxwell's ranch house at Cimarron. Felsenthal's
soldiers escorted the mail here for delivery to Fort Union.
(Courtesy Philmont Boy Scout Ranch)

Felsenthal's Maynard carbine with tape primer manufactured by Massachusetts Arms Company, Chicopee Falls, in 1857. Only 400 of the original models were made and few exist today. (Photograph by Bob Lawrence)

The engraved plaque mounted on the stock of the Maynard carbine carried by Felsenthal during his military service. (Photograph by Bob Lawrence)

Left: Charles Clever, Felsenthal's friend and mentor. Clever, an ambitious, self-made man, was active in merchandising, law, and politics. He wielded considerable influence in Santa Fe for two decades. (Courtesy Museum of New Mexico, Photo Collections)

Right: Bernard Seligman, an influential Santa Fe merchant who, like Felsenthal, was a German-born Jew. The two men were friends for over forty years. (Courtesy Museum of New Mexico, Photo Collections)

Left: Candelario Martinez as he appeared when serving in the New Mexico Infantry Volunteers. Some years later Martinez was called upon to testify in support of Felsenthal's old soldiers pension application. (Courtesy Museum of New Mexico, Photo Collections)

Right: Edward H. Bergmann, former New Mexico volunteer officer, who later became superintendent of the New Mexico penitentiary when it was established in Santa Fe. He gave the only negative deposition of three made by witnesses for Felsenthal's pension hearing. (Courtesy Museum of New Mexico, Photo Collections)

Felsenthal's grave marker at Los Angeles National Cemetery.
(Photograph by Robert L. Meketa)

In October 1861, Captain Felsenthal and his company were released from their duty in the construction of defenses at Fort Union and ordered to march south to Fort Craig to bolster defenses there. They made the more than 280-mile march in about seventeen days and camped outside the fort, slightly to the south of it. They were one of the four New Mexico infantry companies stationed there at the time. Colonel Carson and the rest of the New Mexico Volunteers had not yet arrived and Maj. Arthur Morrison, who, like Felsenthal, was a German Jew, was the ranking officer.[6]

During November and December things remained quiet at the fort and no word came of an advance of the enemy, so Captain Felsenthal, whose company was still short of men, and Major Morrison were ordered to leave Fort Craig to travel to surrounding areas to try to enlist more personnel from the native population. They returned from their recruiting duty on December 27 and shortly thereafter, in January 1862, they were notified that Sibley, now a general, and his army of Texans had crossed into the Territory and were beginning their march north. The war was to begin in earnest.

In January, Colonel Carson, who had been in Albuquerque for some time, left and marched down to Fort Craig with more troops, some of them only recently recruited and poorly trained, to increase the military strength at the fort. By early February there were at least 4,000 Union troops under arms at the post, including regulars, volunteers, militia, and one company of Colorado volunteers. The influx of men, supplies, and horses and mules caused such crowding that many of the troops had to camp outside the walls. Nevertheless, spirits were high and the men seemed confident of victory.

Daily, as the Confederates made their way north, scouts and spy companies were sent southward from Fort Craig to reconnoiter and report back with news of the progress of the Texans. On February 16, and again four days later, units of the First New Mexico Volunteers marched south, pulling cannons with them. On both occasions they fired shots at the approaching Texans but avoided any troop engagement although one Volunteer enlisted man died of wounds from Confederate gunfire. At four o'clock on the afternoon of February 20, when Colonel Canby saw that the Confederates had moved up a ravine in some bluffs on the east side of the river opposite Fort Craig, he dispatched a large force of men across the Rio Grande to attack. But, when the advance guard of Canby's troops was shelled by some of the Texan's cannons, confusion resulted and the Union soldiers were unable to form a satisfactory line. Canby then decided it would be inexpedient to continue the attack, particularly since night was approaching and he left troops in position to prevent the Confederates from moving into any strategically advantageous spot under cover of darkness.

The Confederates desperately needed water, for Canby's troops had effectively blocked them from obtaining any at the river. Early the next morning Sibley was observed moving some of his Texans northward toward a crossing place a few miles distant on the Rio Grande. Canby then ordered several of his units in the same direction on the west side of the river. Soon it became clear that the Confederates were trying to gain control of the ford, called Valverde.[7] The Union forces imme-

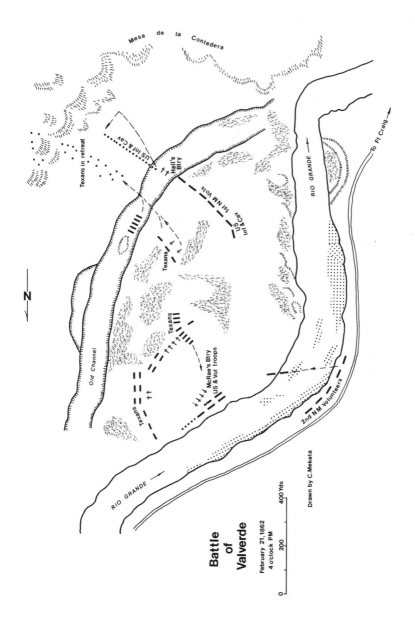

Battle
of
Valverde

February 21, 1862
4 o'clock PM

Drawn by C. Meketa

0	200	400 Yds	

Mesa de la Contedera

Texans in retreat

US Inf & Cav

Hall's Btry

1st NM Vols

US Inf & Cav

Texans

Texans

McRae's Btry
US & Vol troops

Texans

RIO GRANDE

RIO GRANDE

To Ft Craig

2nd NM Volunteers

Old Channel

N

35

diately engaged the advance unit of Confederates, using dismounted cavalrymen on the east side of the river and an artillery barrage from cannons which remained on the west side. After a struggle which lasted a little more than an hour, the southerners were driven back by the Union men. This was the beginning of the bloody conflict now known as the Battle of Valverde.

The furious, all-day fight began with the Union forces on the west side of the river, firing their field pieces and muskets at the Confederates who had the advantage of cover from some sand hills and cottonwood trees on the east bank. Eventually, the commanders of the exposed northern troops ordered an advance and the Union soldiers, on foot and horseback, sprang forward "with a shout" into the chilly waters of the river, described in various personal accounts as from thigh-high to reaching to the men's armpits. As they plunged through the water, the Confederates opened fire, killing many as they attempted the river crossing. However, Canby's men reached the eastern bank of the river and a heated battle then ensued.

The ten companies of Carson's First New Mexico Volunteers fought beside the other Union troops and Captain Felsenthal and his men were in the midst of the action. It was a grisly theater of death with round shot and minie bullets from the small arms making a leaden shower of destruction along with the booming cannons which belched forth both shell and grape. Like all battles it was a terrible mixture of acrid smoke, the screams of wounded men, of blood, and fear, and confusion. At one of the most critical periods in the fighting some of the Confederates used double-barrelled shotguns against their enemies while many of the Volunteer soldiers were armed with only single shot, outdated muskets, which were standard issue for them.[8] Approximately 3,500 men were involved in the battle, with the Confederates slightly outnumbered. Official reports put the number of Union casualties as 68 killed, 160 wounded and 35 missing and the Confederate losses at 36 dead, 150 wounded, and one missing, making the conflict as sanguine as many of the more famous Civil War battles which took place in the East. A number of the wounded were to suffer lingering, painful deaths in the weeks following the attack. Carson's regiment lost one enlisted man, had another wounded, and listed eleven missing. His unit was singled out for commendation by several of the officers who later wrote reports about the battle.

Captain Felsenthal's actions during the fight have not been specifically recorded but, three years later, in a letter written by Charles Clever to Gen. James Carleton, Clever said, "At the Battle of Valverde he [Felsenthal] was conspicuous for courage and bravery."[9]

Later in the afternoon the left wing of the Union forces was overrun, leaving their center exposed, and Canby was forced to order a retreat across the Rio Grande and return his soldiers to the confines of Fort Craig. Although General Canby explained his defeat in part by stating that he received "but little (assistance) from the volunteers," and this accusation was repeated in enough history books to become an accepted fact on the part of many, it is an arguable point, particularly where Carson's First Regiment is concerned. Indignation was expressed by at least one of the First Regiment officers at being ordered to retreat at a time when his troops were pushing the Texans back. Augustus A. Hayes, in *An Unwritten Episode of the Late War*, stated, "One cannot write the history of this remarkable campaign without mentioning the strong opinion of some of Carson's fiery fighters, and even at least one officer of distinction and experience, that victory was within their grasp at Valverde and lost by mismanagement. . . . "[10]

Sibley and his southerners had won the battle, but the Union troops were now holed up in the fort with no intention of surrendering. Early that morning, before the battle had commenced, more than 200 of the Texans' horses and mules had been captured at the river after they had broken loose during the night and rushed to the water to drink. Now forced to abandon many of his wagons for lack of animals and already short of supplies, Sibley realized he could not lay siege to Fort Craig. He decided to bypass it and proceed north to capture sorely needed rations at Albuquerque and Santa Fe. It is probable that Captain Felsenthal and many of the other soldiers, humiliated by the defeat, vowed future revenge as they watched from within the safety of the fort walls and saw the southerners march north.

The victorious Texans made their way to Albuquerque unimpeded, but word of their coming had preceded them. There the Union quartermaster at the post had already loaded the ammunition wagons and sent them northward. He then set fire to the remaining stores that could not be transported and evacuated his troops. Although some of the burning provisions were rescued by a few of the village inhabitants who were sympathetic to the secessionists, there was little in the town to sustain an army and the desperate Confederates then marched sixty miles farther north to Santa Fe. When they arrived they found that the territorial government, the small Union garrison, and most of the supplies had been evacuated to Fort Union.

After a brief, two-day rest in the town, the Texans headed for Fort Union, intending to attack the installation. Unknown to them, 1,300 Colorado volunteer infantrymen were on a forced march, which covered 172 miles through deep snow and over high mountain passes in five days, to reinforce the New Mexico troops at Fort Union. The Colorado soldiers arrived several days before the Confederates could reach Fort Union and on March 26, 1862, the Rebel and Union units met in the mountains east of Santa Fe in the Battle of Glorieta Pass. The Texans were soundly beaten and, demoralized, began a retreat, first to Santa Fe, and then south to Albuquerque.

While all this had been going on General Canby had remained at Fort Craig with his troops. Their first priority, other than treating the wounded, was to reinforce many of the defenses at the post. Much earthwork was done, almost all the men were turned out to dig deep trenches on the east and west sides of the fort and brush was placed around the ramparts, which were mounted with eight cannons. Canby also turned his attention to clarifying and consolidating the records and personnel of the troops under his command. A great deal of confusion existed during and after the battle, with a number of desertions from various units, and Canby needed an organized and cohesive force under his command. On March 3, he ordered that Felsenthal's Company "G" and Company "D", the two most severely undermanned companies in the First

Regiment, transfer their privates to the other companies to bring them up to strength. The officers, noncoms, and musicians were to remain assigned to the cannibalized companies but were sent out on recruiting duties again to sign up volunteers to rebuild their units. By this action Canby would have eight wellstaffed companies in Carson's regiment rather than ten riddled with vacancies.

As a result of these actions, Felsenthal and the other officers of the two companies left Fort Craig to travel northward at the same time the Confederate army was making its way from Albuquerque to Santa Fe. Undoubtedly the men took a more easterly route, heading northward along the river until they made their way through the mountain pass at Abo, then following a trail northeasterly to Anton Chico, and finally northward once again to the vicinity of Fort Union. At any rate, orders show that they were soon recruiting in the area between Santa Fe and Fort Union and were told to work their way eastward, closer to Mora and the fort, as the Confederates advanced, to avoid capture. Felsenthal's exact whereabouts at the time of the Battle of Glorieta cannot be ascertained, but he was probably at Fort Union. At any rate, only a few days after the Texan's defeat, orders were issued at the fort, on April 2, granting a leave of absence to Felsenthal, Major Morrison, and several other officers, probably once again sending them out on recruiting duties.

Meanwhile, on April 1, General Canby, at Fort Craig, took 860 Regular Army soldiers and 350 volunteers, including one company of Colorado men, and marched north. He left Kit Carson and the balance of the New Mexico Volunteers at the fort with instructions to defend it from the Confederates if they retreated south or against any reinforcements that could conceivably appear from Texas.

It was not until Canby's force had reached Socorro that he received word that the Texans had been defeated at Glorieta and were commencing a retreat back to Texas. On April 10 Canby's force began shelling Albuquerque from its southern border in an attempt to dislodge the Confederate troops that had been left behind to secure it. However, after receiving word from some of the town's citizens that the Texans would not allow the civilians to seek refuge from the bombardment of Canby's two 24-pounders, a "cease fire" was ordered. That night, under cover of darkness, Canby's troops secretly marched through Tijeras Canyon to the village of San Antonio, twenty miles east of Albuquerque. There Canby hoped to meet some reinforcements coming from Fort Union. Once the additional troops had arrived, the combined force left on April 14 and marched back to the Rio Grande, to Peralta, twenty miles south of Albuquerque. There, on April 15, Canby's soldiers engaged in a skirmish with the Rebels and in the following days the disorganized retreating Texans were hounded by the Union troops as they made their way down the river.

Fearful of venturing too close to Fort Craig where Carson's Volunteers were waiting, and harassed by Canby's soldiers, the Confederates, now in deplorable condition, turned west near present-day Bernardo. Leaving the easier river route, they struck out across the desert and around the fearful Magdalena Mountains, then turning south and bypassing Fort Craig. By this time they were no longer marching as an army but rather as detached parties of men, desperately short of supplies, trying to make their way back home on their own. The Civil War in New Mexico was over and the Texans had suffered another ignoble defeat. By the time they limped back across the border, their original force of approximately 3,700 had been reduced to slightly more than 1,500 sadly worn men.

Captain Felsenthal must have been somewhat disconcerted by this turn of events. His company had been broken up and he was still out trying to recruit men to refill it. He had relinquished his civilian business pursuits, pledged to serve three years in the military, raised and trained the men of his original company, learned to cope with the rigors of the life of a foot soldier, and now, only nine months later, the Civil War for New Mexicans was finished. But it was not yet time to hang the Maynard on the wall as a memento. New Mexico's problems were not yet solved, and Felsenthal would see more military service but against a very different enemy.

4

Guarding the Santa Fe Trail
1862–1865

While the regular and volunteer troops had been preoccupied with fighting off the invading Texans, the Navajos and Apaches took advantage of their absence to step up their raids on livestock herds and against settlers and prospectors. The Indians, angered by the continued intrusions into their lands, had become so active that they were now virtually in control of large areas of New Mexico. While no figures are available for the 1861–62 period, one report stated that in 1863 Indian depredations had caused 80 deaths, 38 woundings, and the theft of 748 horses, 3,626 head of cattle, 42,044 sheep, 254 mules, 2,075 goats, 78 burros, and 2,103 other animals.[1] The territorial and federal officials decided that they would use the military force they now had organized and available to mount a campaign against the Indians to try to crush them.

The military authorities realized, however, that foot soldiers would be ineffective against the wide-ranging Indians and that a cavalry would be needed. Therefore, in May 1862, shortly after the ragged Texan troops had quit the Territory, the First Regiment, New Mexico Infantry was disbanded and many officers and men were mustered out as a reorganization took place. Some personnel from the First, Second, Fourth, and Fifth Regiments of the New Mexico Volunteers were consolidated to form the new First Regiment Cavalry (Volunteers). More officers than needed were available, and during the reorganization Louis Felsenthal was dropped from the official rolls and discharged against his wishes, either because of a clerical error due to the confusion of the mass reassignments or because some other captain with more influence obtained one of the ten slots open for that rank. Whatever the reason, Felsenthal was hurt, angry, and indignant at this turn of events and took immediate action to try to rectify it. He was now back in Santa Fe and enlisted the aid of some very influential people in his attempt to reenter the military. He was even willing to accept a lower rank. On June 5, 1862, a letter signed by Governor Henry Connelly, Charles Clever, and O. P. Hovey was sent to General Canby recommending that Louis Felsenthal be given a position of first lieutenant in any of the companies being added to the new cavalry regiment.[2] It seems strange that Governor Connelly would be recommending Felsenthal to General Canby for a commission, since Connelly himself was the person who made the appointments. Perhaps this was the protocol of the time, however, with no appointments being made unless General Canby approved them. This would appear to be the procedure, for on July 8, Felsenthal wrote a letter to General Canby requesting that he recommend him to the governor for a commission in some of the additional companies being formed. In it he wrote:

I raised my Company at great trouble and expense to myself, and much of that expense has never been reimbursed to me. My Company was broken up in March[3] and I myself ordered on recruiting services, but in reality, instead of having an opportunity of filling my Company again, I was kept upon detached service, until I was mustered out of service on the 31st of May. My Muster Rolls and other papers have all been attended to and I now find myself thrown out of all employment after having relinquished all my business pursuits for the purpose of entering the service of the U.S. during the War.[4]

Felsenthal had good reason to be upset: when he had signed the Muster-In-Rolls nine months earlier he had been commissioned a captain for a period of three years, and he must have made plans to serve for that period of time; however, now he seemed to have been betrayed by the government with which he had entered into the contract.

For reasons that are unclear, however, Felsenthal failed to obtain the appointment he was requesting, in spite of the efforts of his prominent friends. His strongest advocate appeared to be Charles Clever who, some years later, referred to Felsenthal's dismissal from the service as a mistake. In a letter to General Carleton in 1865, Clever said:

Through some misunderstanding—when the two regiments were consolidated—he was dropped from the list of Officers. At that time, many of his friends and among them regular and volunteer officers of the highest standing, regretted this occurrence and were unanimous in expressing the opinion that the action taken against him was undeserved and erroneous. General Canby, the then Commander of the Department, assured me that he was extremely sorry that Captain Felsenthal had been dropped and would readily rectify the error, which had happened through misconception were it in his powers to do so.[5]

The governor's recommendation, the general's expressed regrets, and the appeals by Felsenthal and his friends all failed to reestablish Felsenthal as a military officer. Forced to find civilian employment, he obtained a job at the military headquarters in Santa Fe. However, he obviously felt that he had been treated very badly by the army. Not only had he spent some of his personal funds in the recruiting effort, which the military had not paid back, but to make matters worse, at the time of his discharge he had not even been paid his captain's salary for six of the nine months he had served. Pay records for the last day of May 1862, the date of his discharge, showed that the last reimbursement he had received had been in November 1861.[6] Now he had been ignobly cast aside and his men, in effect, stolen to be incorporated into other companies in the reorganized cavalry.

Evidently in pique, Captain Felsenthal retained some of the records of his former company. Perhaps he felt that the records should be his, but his action resulted in a complaining letter written by Colonel Carson to the assistant adjutant general of the department headquarters in Santa Fe. In the August 27, 1862 letter, Carson said that in several instances company commanders had complained to him because they were unable to obtain the Descriptive Rolls of men transferred to them from the "late" company of Captain Felsenthal. He said, "Captain Felsenthal has been repeatedly written to from these Headquarters to furnish the necessary Descriptive Rolls, but it seems he has failed to do so."[7] Carson closed by requesting that the department commander give orders which would compel Felsenthal to comply. No records exist to show whether Felsenthal capitulated, but this minor incident was a precursor to future problems Felsenthal would have about the retention of military records.

So, during the balance of 1862 and part of 1863, Louis Felsenthal remained an unwilling civilian. During that time, Kit Carson and the First New Mexico Cavalry were warring against the marauding Indians in several portions of the Territory, conducting a campaign of relentless pursuit and harsh punishment. By March 1863, Carson had subjugated the Mescalero Apaches in south-central New Mexico, and they had been moved to a new reservation at the Bosque Redondo in the eastern part of the Territory. In June of that year Carson and his troops were ordered to march west to pit their force against the Navajos.

However, while the soldiers were tied up with these campaigns, the Kiowas and Comanches were striking viciously at the Santa Fe Trail and the settlements on the eastern fringes of New Mexico. In the south, westward from the Rio Grande into Arizona, the southern Apaches of the Mimbres, Gila, Mogollon, and Chiricahua tribes had practically immobilized all attempts to settle, mine, or even travel through the area. More troops were obviously needed and in the summer of 1863 plans were made to raise a new regiment, this time of infantrymen. On September 21, Governor Connelly issued a proclamation authorizing the establishment of ten new companies, which would make up the regiment. This was the opportunity Louis Felsenthal was waiting for. He applied for, and was granted, a commission, but the matter was not as simple as it sounds. The commission was only to recruit, and he would not officially become an officer until he once again raised a company.

Once granted the commission, Felsenthal was required to report to Maj. Henry R. Selden, superintendent of the recruiting service, for instructions. He, like the other potential officers, was told that he could rent a room "at the most reasonable rates" in the area where he intended to raise his men, and use it as a place of rendezvous. They were further instructed that each should, "by his personal exertions, and such announcements as may be proper and legal, proceed to recruit men for his Company, and collect them at his rendezvous."[8] Each time they obtained approximately six volunteers, the officers were to send them on to a "General Rendezvous" where the men would be given physical examinations and mustered in if found acceptable. Once half a company of "physically and morally fit" men (or a total of about forty) had been mustered in, a first lieutenant could be sworn in. It was not until a minimum number, eighty men, had been mustered in, that a company captain and second lieutenant would become official officers. If a sufficient number of men to fill the company had not been raised "within a reasonable time," those men already signed up would be transferred to other companies of the regiment and the recruiting officer would be out of luck. Felsenthal and the others were exhorted to keep costs to a minimum and were told they must present receipts showing their personal outlay of money used in subsistence and transportation of recruits if they wished to be reimbursed. By February 23, 1864, Felsenthal had succeeded in recruiting enough men and was mustered in as a captain, commanding Company "C".

Felsenthal, of course, did not do all the recruiting personally. One of his first actions was to recruit Andres Tapia of Santa Fe, who had served as a second lieutenant in Company "F" in the old infantry and who had fought at the Battle of Valverde against the Texans. Tapia had been retained in the service during the reorganization after the defeat of the Confederates and served for a short time in Company "B" of Carson's cavalry. However, by September 10, 1862, Tapia had been dismissed from the service after being found guilty of the charge of conduct unbecoming an officer and a gentleman.[9]

By an obvious prior agreement with Felsenthal, Tapia began recruiting men for Company "C" on December 7, 1863, and by January 21, enough men had been signed up for him to be commissioned as the company's first lieutenant. The company's second lieutenant was José Trujillo, also an experienced military man, who had been a second lieutenant in Major José Sena's Company "B," Second Regiment, New Mexico Volunteers (Old), which participated in the Battle of Valverde in 1862. Most of the company's men were recruited from northern New Mexico and the Santa Fe area, and the men processed for induction at Fort Marcy in the capital city.

The completion of the roster of men for the company must have been a moment of great personal satisfaction for Felsenthal. He was once more authorized to wear the uniform of the Union Army and the officer's insignia which showed him to be a leader of men. He had overcome what he felt was an undeserved and ignominious rejection by the military, and he had done it the hard way—raising an entire company of men for the second time.

On February 26, three days after Captain Felsenthal and Lieutenant Trujillo had received their commissions, the company was posted to Fort Union, arriving there on March 1. The company's job would be to provide escort service for the U.S. mail, the wagon trains, and the herds of cattle coming over the Santa Fe Trail. This was the most perilous year the Trail had ever seen. The Kiowas and Comanches had grown increasingly bold and troublesome as they took advantage of the preoccupation of the Territorial soldiers with the campaign against the Navajos to the west. They began to attack the wagon trains with frequency, taking a fearful toll of lives and property from the caravans while they were between the Fort Larned, Kansas, and Fort Union.

The escort duty carried out by infantry companies such as Felsenthal's was hazardous, physically demanding, and filled with hardships so great it is difficult to understand what motivated these men to volunteer into military service to endure them. As infantrymen they walked enormous distances alongside the lumbering wagons of the trains. A typical trip might be from Fort Union in northeastern New Mexico to Fort Lyon, Colorado, and then on to Fort Larned, Kansas, a distance of approximately 600 miles, which took almost a month. Privates were paid thirteen dollars a month and Captain Felsenthal earned seventy dollars as com-

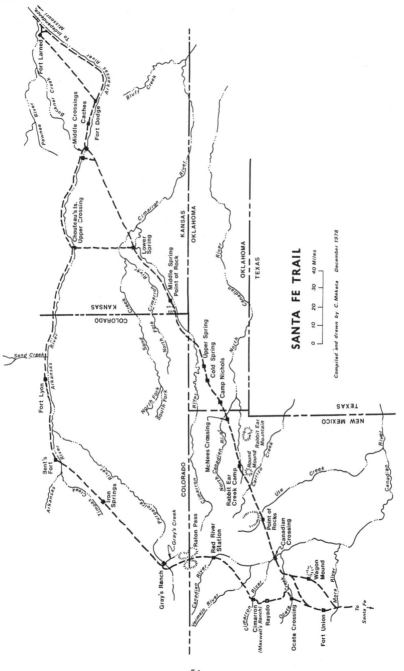

SANTA FE TRAIL

Compiled and drawn by C. Maketa   December 1978

0   10   20   30   40 Miles

51

pany commander. On occasions, bad weather could be as much a danger to the troops as the menacing Indians.

During the summer of 1864, the Indians became more daring and successful in their raids. By the end of August, Fort Union found itself practically encircled by the marauders. That month Gen. James Carleton, commander of the Department of New Mexico, wrote to Washington to notify them that he had ordered units of volunteer soldiers, cavalry and infantry, to five locations on the Santa Fe Trail in an attempt to guard the road. He took this action based in part on a letter he had received from a Col. J. C. McFerran who had just arrived in Santa Fe, having come over the mail route from Kansas City, Missouri. In the letter, Colonel McFerran said that "every tribe that frequents the plains is engaged in daily depredations on the trains, and immense losses to the Government and individuals have occurred, and many lives have already been lost."[10] McFerran stated that the Comanches, Cheyennes, Kiowas, Arapahoes, and Apaches of the plains were "all combined in these most brutal outrages" and added that "soldiers and citizens have been killed within sight of a large number of troops" and "women and children have been taken prisoners to suffer treatment worse than death."

Captain Felsenthal's company was one of those General Carleton detailed to strategic sites on the Trail. On August 28, 1864, they received orders to begin several month's duty providing escort service for the U.S. mails between several points on the more northerly Mountain Branch of the Santa Fe Trail. Felsenthal and his men were to camp on the banks of the Purgatory River in southern Colorado, near Gray's Ranch, a site about four miles east of present-day Trinidad. From this point they could provide escort services to Lucien B. Maxwell's Ranch sixty-seven miles to the south and northward to Fort Lyon, about 120 miles away.

This assignment required the soldiers to traverse Raton Canyon on their way south to Maxwell's Ranch where there was a mill, a mail station, and a store. The twenty-five-mile-long road through the canyon was very bad, wagons often had extreme difficulty getting through, but water could usually be found at several places along the route. When the mail was safely delivered to Maxwell's Ranch, it would be met by other troops from Fort Union who would guard it on its final leg of the dangerous journey to the fort. Felsenthal and the men of Company "C" were aware of the perilous conditions of this duty because Indian attacks at different points along the Trail had become an almost daily affair. Conditions had become so bad that many contractors and private trains were corralled and unable to move from their camps. In that month, reports told of one large wagon train from which all the livestock had been stolen by a roving band of Indians. The train was stranded and unable to move until army animals were dispatched from Fort Larned to bring it back to safety.

A much more grisly fate befell a citizen train captured on August 19 on the Cimarron River. In a report made at Fort Larned, Maj. Scott Anthony said, "The train was entirely destroyed (burned) by the Indians and all the white men with it were killed and their bodies most horribly mutilated, heads cut off, hearts cut out, and evidently placed in the center of their 'dance circle' while they held their fiendish war dance around them, and kicked the mutilated bodies about the prairies."[11] Major Anthony also reported much trouble "further up the river, near Fort Lyon," the area to which Felsenthal's company was enroute. Anthony said that several soldiers and citizens had been murdered there and two women carried off by small bands of Indians. Even government trains on their way to Fort Union were attacked on the twenty-first of the month.[12]

It was under these conditions, then, that Captain Felsenthal and Company "C" marched to their duty station and set up rough camp on the banks of the Purgatory. The next two months would prove to be extremely unpleasant, but not primarily because of the Indians.

Felsenthal's first problem was caused by the "stealing" of his limited supply of men and equipment by the commanding officer of Fort Lyon who, fearful of the hostile Indians, was attempting to increase the strength of his garrison by retaining Felsenthal's men each time they arrived at his post after escorting the mail there. Under the standing orders, these men were supposed to escort the next southbound mail delivery back and return to Felsenthal's small and dangerously exposed troop. By October 20, Felsenthal was so angry about the pilfering of men from his modest command, he wrote to the post adjutant of Fort Union to complain and ask for help, saying,

regardless to the Orders I give to the Non-commissioned Officers of detachments I send to Fort Lyon as Escorts to the U.S. Mail, generally said detachments are retained at

Ft. Lyon, and treated as a Company there.—Most of the Transportation, for which I am responsible is now at Ft. Lyon, and I do not know, what has or will become of the same. My provisions is [sic] nearly out and if matters go on this way, my Company will soon be at Ft. Lyon and I with my first Sergeant and buglers, will be left alone to guard the Camp and Escort the Mails. [13]

Felsenthal's sarcasm was understandable. Not only was his company being plundered of its strength by the commander of Fort Lyon, but his second-in-command, 1st Lt. Andres Tapia, was so ill that Felsenthal was obliged to send him, lying in the bed of a wagon, to Fort Union for medical attention. While Felsenthal was able to send the complaining letter along with Lieutenant Tapia, the necessity of returning the officer to Fort Union further depleted his strength for he was obliged to send a sergeant, three privates, some recruits he had obtained, ten day's provisions and a six-mule team along to escort the sick man back to assure his safe arrival. Now Felsenthal would have to rely heavily on his first sergeant, a thirty-nine-year-old Pole from Warsaw, Boniface Machowitz, who, being five foot ten, was considerably taller than his commanding officer. [14]

Conditions were becoming intolerable. Not only were his few men exposed to hazards both on escort duty and in camp, but the weather was increasingly troublesome. In the same letter to Fort Union, Felsenthal described their living conditions:

I am encamped here on the River, without any other shelter, than a few brush-huts, the days, and especially the nights are very cold, and we have snow-storms here every few days, in consequence of which the men, (they having but little clothing) are suffering very much.

Felsenthal went on to say that he was almost out of provisions; that two of his mules had died, the rest were nearly exhausted, and that he felt that two more escort trips would leave him without any animals. At this point only about six more days remained of the two months his company had been detailed to serve at Gray's Ranch. It was, however, not until the twenty-ninth of the month that the command left their camp and began the march back to Fort Union. The company, or the remnants of it, probably set off in good humor, looking forward to the relative creature comforts of duty at the fort. But things were not to be that easy.

The route the company had to take back would require them to traverse Raton Pass, whose almost 8,000-foot elevation has always made it a treacherous place during any of the months when sudden mountain snowstorms can surprise travelers. During this march, Captain Felsenthal's leadership qualities, stamina, and courage were severely tested as can be seen from a letter he wrote on November 9 from Rayado, New Mexico, to the commanding officer of Fort Union. The simple report poignantly illustrates the physical hardships and struggles of his men:

I left Gray's Ranch with my Company on the 29th of October last. On arriving at the foot of the summit of Raton Pass, we were caught in a severe snow storm. Under great difficulties we got to Red River Station that day. It snowed all that night, and the next morning, the snow on the level ground measured 19 inches deep, snowing still, and continuing so all day long. I remained at Red River Station for two days, but there being no forage, nor shelter for either men or beasts, I concluded to march on, to some place, where I might obtain both. It took us four days & very hard labor to come from Red River Station to Mr. Maxwell's Ranch and not being able to obtain there what we needed, we proceeded to Rayado where we arrived two days ago. For miles and miles the Company had to march through snow which reached to their waist-belts, and had even then to assist in pulling, and pushing the wagons. I was fortunate enough to lose no mules, but they are utterly exhausted and need good rest and care, before I will be able to proceed. Many of my men had part of their feet frozen, and the majority got snowblind.[15]

Felsenthal further explained in the letter that he had "46 Enlisted Men, 4 Quarter Masters [sic] Teamsters and two Laundresses, four Wagons & 23 Government Animals"[16] with him at the ranch of a Mr. Jesús Abreu who had given them shelter, food, and stables for the animals. He also mentioned that he had been able to buy 378 pounds of beef to feed his men from a Mr. W. Jones of Denver who had been caught in the same storm while driving a herd of cattle destined for Fort Union. Felsenthal closed the letter by asking for instructions from the Fort Union post adjutant as to how he wished him to proceed.

Four days later he received some rations for his men from Fort Union, but no instructions. He wrote to the adjutant again the next day, suggesting that the post send him fresh mules and allow him to leave the others in Mr. Abreu's stables saying, "I sincerely believe to loose [sic] every Mule I have with me, if I should undertake a trip with them now, in their present state of exhaustion and on a road in a condition to kill fresh and healthy animals."[17] Felsenthal also said that while writing the letter he had received notice that sixteen men, two wagons, and eight mules he had left behind at Fort Lyon, probably some of those he had been complaining about earlier, had arrived at a spot eight miles away and were expected to join him the next day. He described them as being in "a deplorable condition."

There is no further documentation available describing the balance of the trip but Felsenthal and Company "C" eventually returned safely to Fort Union. Their exploits were probably considered nothing out of the ordinary by the other troops since danger and discomfort were daily burdens to the army men in the Territory.

During the balance of the 1864–65 winter, Captain Felsenthal and Company "C" remained at Fort Union. They were kept busy with duties both on and off the post. Felsenthal and other company commanders did inventories of stores, sent their men out on short trips in the surrounding countryside and towns to search for and apprehend deserters, drilled the troops weekly in military tactics, and handled the mountains of reports and other paperwork always involved in army procedures. The enlisted men also helped with major construction being done on the fort at that time and escorted messengers carrying dispatches to other installations.

In early February 1865, the commanding officer of Fort Union, Col. Henry R. Selden of the Infantry

Volunteers, died after a short illness. After a solemn funeral and full military honors, he was buried at the fort.[18] Official orders were issued requiring all officers to wear the prescribed badge of mourning for a thirty-day period.

Lt. Col. Francisco Abreu, also of the Volunteers and brother of the man who had provided Felsenthal's men a haven during the snowstorm, was made a full colonel and promoted to fill the vacancy left by Colonel Selden's death. As a result of several promotions, the rank of major became open. Either on his own or at Felsenthal's instigation, Charles Clever, who was in Santa Fe, went to see Governor Connelly to recommend that Felsenthal be promoted. The governor, who had the power to make the appointment, told Clever that he would consider any of the men recommended by General Carleton, commander of the Department of New Mexico. Clever had wasted no time, for on February 21, only about eighteen days after Selden's death, he wrote the general a letter that was strongly complimentary of Felsenthal. In it he not only requested that Felsenthal be considered for the promotion, but cited his previous exemplary service during the Battle of Valverde and stated that had it not been for the unfair and unfortunate circumstance of Felsenthal's earlier dismissal from the military, he would have probably already achieve the rank of major like many of his contemporaries. However, all Clever's influence and efforts were in vain; General Carleton eventually gave another captain the promotion.

The general clearly had more momentous matters than the promotion to consider at that time. He was making plans to protect caravans along the Santa Fe

Trail during the 1865 travel season. He published a notice to put into effect a method he had devised whereby a company of troops would be made available on the first and fifteenth of each month to escort wagon trains from Fort Union to Fort Larned, Kansas. Once the troops had safely escorted a train to Fort Larned, they would remain there until a westward traveling train had been assembled and then escort it back. This ambitious escort system was put into effect in March, but it put such a drain on Carleton's limited manpower that he had to discontinue the service after only a few months. But before it was stopped, Captain Felsenthal and Company "C" were called upon to undertake one of the trips.

Each of the infantry companies of Volunteers was sent on the escort duty in scheduled rotation; hence, Felsenthal was aware that he and his men would leave in April. In March he requested a two-week leave of absence to travel to Santa Fe to attend to personal business. Possibly one of the items on his agenda was a lobbying attempt to secure the promotion to major, but the one concrete memento of his trip to the city is an old tintype photograph of him, with four other officers, which appears to have been taken in a rather primitive studio adorned with canvas backdrop and a jerga carpet. [19]

On April 15, Company "C" was ordered to escort a train via the Cimarron Cutoff to Fort Larned. A copy of their Special Orders paints a graphic picture of the conditions under which the trip was made:

Every officer and effective man will go. It (the company) will take 100 rounds of ammunition per man in boxes, and twenty rounds per man in their cartridge boxes. Each man will be allowed to take 2 blankets, 1 great coat, 2 extra shirts, 2 extra drawers, 1 pr. extra shoes, 1 pr. extra pants, and no more clothing except what he wears. Owing to the state of the roads between here and Fort Larned the company will be rationed to include the 15th of May.

Captain Felsenthal is expected to look out well for the safety of the animals and property he is to escort and guard. It is hoped that he and his company will not only be ready to fight but will fight any number of hostile Indians they may meet or who may attack or menace the company or the trains, by night or by day, in storm or in fine weather. It is hoped that neither Officers nor men will be off their guard or idle away their time, but will attend to the business for which they are paid.

No man's musket will be carried in a wagon. He must carry it himself all the time.

Two tents only will be taken by the Company.

Two wagons will be allowed for transportation.[20]

Captain Felsenthal and Company "C" made the long trip to Fort Larned without major problems and it was probably not until their arrival there that they learned the devastating news of President Lincoln's death. When the news had reached Santa Fe on May 5, a deep gloom had settled over the populace. Homes and buildings had been hung with heavy draperies, dark emblems of death, and the following Sunday the sad and mournful silence had been broken every half hour by the deep roar of cannons from Fort Marcy.

In June, Company "C" was assigned to guard a large train for the return trek to Fort Union. The train, headed by a man named Kitchen, had 145 wagons and a large herd of cattle. About midnight, on June 6, the encamped party was attacked by approximately 200 Indians west of Fort Dodge, Kansas. Although Felsenthal had set up pickets around the train and there were also herders and mayordomos with the animals, the Indians managed to stampede 1,200 head of the cattle being escorted.

One picket, under command of a corporal, however, did attack the Indians and impede their escape until Felsenthal, with a platoon of men, could arrive at the scene of action. On the approach of the captain, the Indians fled and the soldiers chased them for eight miles, continually firing their weapons at the retreating Indians. Although considerable skirmishing took place, because of the darkness of the night, it could not be determined whether or not any of the rustlers were killed. All but forty-six of the cattle were recovered, and some of those had been shot by the Indians.

For a short time thereafter there were rumors in army circles that the train had been captured, but Captain Felsenthal and his men brought it safely to Fort Union. In a report of the incident, published in the July 29, 1865, issue of the *Santa Fe Weekly Gazette*, Felsenthal is quoted as having said that it was generally believed that there were Texans or bushwhackers among the Indians.

Once back at the post, Felsenthal resumed his routine garrison duties. Among the papers requiring his attention was a General Order, issued by the army, which required officers to state, in writing, whether they desired to remain in the military service. With the conclusion of the Civil War in the East, the United States government was beginning to reduce its man-

power. Although the situation was different in New
Mexico, with the soldiers battling Indians instead of
Rebels, the order was all-inclusive, with no consideration given to the fact that the troops in New Mexico
were still actively involved in confrontations with hostile enemies.

Shortly after Felsenthal returned to Fort Union he
wrote a letter, in compliance with the order, requesting that he no longer be retained in the U.S. military.
His reasons for this action can only be conjectured.
Certainly he must have been disappointed at not receiving the promotion he obviously had hoped for, and it
is probable that he saw no future for himself in the
army. It is also possible that he found that eighteen
months of fighting snowstorms and Indians was enough
and that the glamour attached to the wartime army
had not carried over into peacetime. He would soon
be thirty-three years old; he had vindicated himself of
the stigma of the unwanted discharge of 1862; and
many of his old friends were now out of the military
and back in Santa Fe pursuing civilian interests.

Ironically, Felsenthal was to have almost as much
trouble getting out of the army as he had getting in.
He waited a month and a half for some communication or action on his letter requesting that he be mustered out but heard nothing. So, on the first day of
September 1865, he wrote another letter, this time
tendering a resignation of his commission. In it he
stated that since he had seen other officers of his
regiment receive quick approvals of their muster-out
requests, he had assumed he too would get one. In
anticipation of such action he said he had "made arrangements to enter into the mercantile business by

buying a quantity of goods" and that to be "retained in the Service would therefore involve me in serious inconvenience."[21]

Twelve days after he had posted this letter of resignation, he finally received an answer to the muster-out request. It was refused. Again Felsenthal's plans were being thwarted by an uncooperative military establishment. He immediately replied to this letter, reiterating his desire to resign.

Several factors were working against Felsenthal in his request for a speedy dismissal. An unexpectedly large number of officers had asked to be mustered out once the option had been offered to them in the General Order. Also, the Kiowas and Comanches were still a problem along the Santa Fe Trail and in addition, Navajos and Apaches had been escaping from the Bosque Redondo on the banks of the Pecos River in eastern New Mexico where they had been incarcerated after their earlier capture in 1864. The escapees were raiding settlements along the southern portion of the Rio Grande, stealing stock, and even kidnapping or killing villagers. In addition, the Apaches in southwestern New Mexico and in Arizona remained unconquered and troublesome so the military could not indiscriminately muster out all those officers who desired to be discharged.

Moreover, U.S. Army Headquarters in Washington had just ordered an enormous reorganization that abolished the Department of New Mexico, demoting it to a military district under the jurisdiction of the Department of California headquartered in San Francisco. Unfortunately for Felsenthal, this action coincided almost exactly with his request to be discharged. The

Santa Fe headquarters was in a state of turmoil because of the slowness of communications from the East and their uncertainty of their status as evinced by a letter written by General Carleton to the Army Adjutant General on August 5, 1865:

Have seen in newspapers General Orders, No. 118, assigning New Mexico to Department of California. The official order will doubtless come by next mail in twelve days. Between the date of receipt by me of the official order and the date when instructions will be received from General McDowell there will be an hiatus of uncertain duration. In that hiatus this will be no department. What will it be? I see dilemmas with reference to approving contracts, estimates for money, discharges of soldiers, accepting resignations, action with reference to courts-martial, military commissions, etc. I wish to act authoritatively. Please instruct me by telegraph. Expressmen will wait at Denver.

Eventually Felsenthal's request, with a favorable endorsement, would be sent through channels. It would be many months before it would be approved, however, and it would have acquired numerous endorsements and have been sent to both St. Louis, Missouri, and San Francisco, California.

However, Felsenthal had put himself in an uncomfortable position by his premature business venture. He now requested a leave to go to Santa Fe as soon as possible on private business. The leave was granted and on September 19, 1865, while in the city Felsenthal again went to a photographer, this time to have a portrait made. In this sitting, though, he wore a dark suit rather than his uniform.

Meanwhile, the work of the Army had to go on.

General Carleton ordered five companies of men to forts in the southern part of the Territory because the Mimbres Apaches were attacking settlers and stealing stock in the area. Soon after Felsenthal returned to Fort Union, at the end of October, his company was ordered to report to Fort Craig, the scene of Felsenthal's only military battle. Incorporated in his orders were instructions "to attack and destroy all Apache or Navajo men able to bear arms who are found off the Bosque Redondo reservation without passports."[23] The infantrymen were further instructed to take prisoner any Indian women they encountered and to keep a strong guard on their own stock as they traveled southward. It took fifteen days to march to Fort Craig, and Felsenthal and his men were given a ten-day lay-over and then ordered farther down the Rio Grande to take post at Fort McRae. Army records show that the hostile Indians were so bold in the area at that time that they frequently attacked and plundered in close proximity to the forts.

While stationed at Fort McRae, Felsenthal wrote another official letter in which he allowed a mild sarcasm to surface. Obviously irritated by a lieutenant at Fort Craig who was a stickler for paperwork but unable to use his common sense, Felsenthal wrote: "Herewith I have the honor to transmit the original and corrected Return of my Company for the month of March last. By referring to the aggregate number of enlisted men *you might easily have seen,* that my Company has all the law for organizing Companies allows it: that is to say 5 Sergeants, 8 Corporals and 2 Musicians."[24] In the same letter Felsenthal replied to the lieutenant's request for information about a former enlisted man who had been in Felsenthal's company before his discharge. Explaining that he had never had the particulars in his records, but that they were probably in the lieutenant's own files, Felsenthal turned the tables saying, "and I would request, in order to complete my Company Descriptive Books, that *you* will send *me* the dates of said Thompson's discharge."

It was at Fort McRae that Captain Felsenthal finally received notification that his resignation had been approved and an honorable discharge issued at Headquarters, Military Division of the Mississippi, in St. Louis on November 25. However, it had taken more than a month for the official papers to arrive, so Felsenthal was not relieved from duty at Fort McRae until the last day of the year. He would begin 1866 as a civilian. In the orders relieving Felsenthal from duty, the post commandant expressed a desire that "the esteem and regard which the Officers and Men have expressed for Captain Louis Felsenthal" be placed on record and added his personal regret that the Captain was leaving the post and the service.[25] He further included "kindest wishes for his (Felsenthal's) future prosperity."

The Commandant's letter combined with an incident which took place at Fort McRae about five months after Felsenthal's departure, raise some provocative questions about Felsenthal's character, First of all, the letter appears to be more than just a polite, routine tribute to a departing officer, for the files of other officers in the regiment do not contain similar missives. It can apparently be inferred, then, that Felsenthal was on very good terms with Capt. William French, the California volunteer officer who commanded the post.

Captain French, however, was castigated by Capt. Frank Harder, the officer who replaced Felsenthal as commander of Company "C". Harder, after the shooting death of one of the Company "C" men in May 1866, wrote a letter to General Carleton who was a personal friend of his. In it he said that for a long period, even prior to his arrival at Fort McRae, it had been the custom of the officers stationed there to indulge in drunken sprees that frequently lasted several nights and days. Harder also charged that, in the time period after Felsenthal's departure, he had observed the enlisted men freely mingling with the officers, on many occasions vying with them over who could drink the most whiskey, and that the sprees generally ended in a row, particularly after one of the Company "C" officers brought a local woman to the post to live with him. [26]

Can it be assumed that the regret expressed by Captain French over Felsenthal's departure from the post was that of a fellow-carouser; that Felsenthal was less military, less conscientious, less disciplined than the other military officers on duty in the Territory at the time? Or did Captain Harder, upset by the untimely death of his man, and perhaps trying to impress General Carleton with his own high moral and military standards, exaggerate conditions at Fort McRae?

The facts are these. Fort McRae, only three-years-old, was a small primitive post garrisoned by only two companies and commanded by lower-ranking officers. It probably was less disciplined than larger facilities. But drunkenness, brawls, and shootings, involving both officers and enlisted men, were common throughout the entire military district during this time. Alcohol was the remedy used to combat the pain of everything from toothache to rheumatic twinges and was the antidote against cold, loneliness, boredom, fatigue, limited diet, and fear.

No doubt Felsenthal, like the others, partook of the bottled "spirits" on many an occassion, but a comparison of his service record with those of many of the other company grade officers of the New Mexico Infantry Volunteers is very flattering. Unlike many of his peers, Felsenthal was never reprimanded for nor had charges of drunkenness or misconduct brought against him. He appeared to be competent in handling his men under a variety of adverse conditions and to have had a strong sense of responsibility. It is entirely possible that the commandant's letter was more than just a polite tribute.

Although they had neither the military background nor the training of Regular Army officers, the men who received commissions in the Volunteers were expected to measure up, in every way, to the standards already set for military commanders. Felsenthal, like the other company commanders, had to fill a variety of roles and be good at all of them. He had to function as leader, physician, priest, and father to the men of his company, commanding their respect and obedience by trying to strike a balance between kindness and firmness, all the while functioning within the narrow confines of Army rules and regulations. While on the long weary marches and in the isolation of wilderness settings, only his good judgment stood between the loss of lives and equipment and the safety of all that was deemed his responsibility.

He was burdened by a complicated system of accountability for a large amount of public property, animals, arms, tools, fuel, and food, and was responsible for correctly maintaining a running account with all the men under his command. In addition, the bureaucratic mountain of paperwork necessary to document every incident or action had to be precisely rendered according to the Army's regulations, for the military was and is a little world within itself.

Regardless of conditions, which could range from insufficient or incompetent personnel to ineffective weapons, Felsenthal and the other company commanders were expected to perform minor miracles regularly and no excuses were acceptable. The pressures were great. And always looming in the background, if a man succumbed to drink, dishonesty, or unacceptable behavior brought on by rage or frustration, was the most damning and morale shattering blow to a man's honor, the charge of "conduct unbecoming an officer and gentleman." Conviction on that indictment would stain a man's reputation for the rest of his life. Louis Felsenthal seemed to be very professional in his career as a soldier and much impressed by the responsibilities incumbent upon those who were privileged to wear the slender glittering sword of the officer.

On the New Year's Day 1866, Louis Felsenthal left the soldier's life behind and headed north to the city where his heart and his home lay—The City of the Holy Faith, Santa Fe. He did not know it then, but ahead of him lay honors and insults, good times and bad, and more battles, not military this time, but legal.

5

An Esteemed Citizen
1866–1880

The beginning of 1866 marked a change in the direction in Louis Felsenthal's life that paralleled a change taking place in Santa Fe and the New Mexico Territory. He had left behind him the role of warrior and military defender at a time when New Mexico was entering a transitional period marked by a strong emphasis on economic development and the rapid arrival of technology from the East. He had served through the heavy Indian depredations of the Santa Fe Trail during 1864 and 1865 and the climax of its military protection. Although army escorts would be a fixture on the Trail for a few more years to guard against occasional bloody attacks, and even though Santa Fe was shocked by rumors, in July 1867, that Bishop Lamy had been killed by Indians near the Arkansas River, the perils of travel on the Trail were diminishing.[1] The advance of the railhead westward and other factors would push the remaining hostile Indians away from the locale of the Santa Fe Trail, and they would never again constitute such a dire threat to those wishing to come to Santa Fe.

Although Santa Fe still retained its frontier flavor, earmarked by occasional drunken brawls, shootings, stock rustlings, and even "lady knife fights,"[2] civilization was making inroads. Livestock was beginning as a dominant industry now that conditions were safer. This was the year that Charles Goodnight and Oliver Loving would bring the first of many herds of Texas cattle up to the Fort Sumner area on the eastern border of New Mexico. The same year a chapter of the Masons would be instituted in Santa Fe; and by the next, gold would be discovered in Colfax county; and peonage would be formally abolished by an act of Congress.

In the first few years following the close of the Civil War, much the same group of influential, wealthy, and important men who had controlled the political and economic features of prewar life in Santa Fe continued to run the town's affairs, many stepping right back into their roles upon their return from the military. These were Felsenthal's contemporaries and those who were not friends were at least acquaintances. They shared the bond of having been pioneer residents of the Territorial period and of having protected and safeguarded New Mexico against both Indians and Confederates. Within this society Felsenthal could be assured of respect, friendships, and many opportunities to make a living.

But change was in the future, slow at first but gradually accelerating. Change that would dilute the power of the older clique and impact on Felsenthal's life. Almost immediately after peace had been declared, maneuvering for political and economic power increased in Santa Fe. On July 16, 1866, Governor Henry Connelly died and was succeeded by Robert B. Mitchell, a political appointee. In September, General Carleton was removed as military commander, to the delight of a large anti-Carleton faction in the Territory. Thus, in a very brief period, the two men who had dominated all facets of Territorial life the preceding few years were gone.

The size and composition of New Mexico's population also began to change with an influx of new settlers. Most were former soldiers whose spirit of adventure had been honed, horizons broadened, and knowledge increased by their military service; men who felt the New Mexico Territory was fertile ground for a new start.

In an 1867 report, Bishop Lamy estimated that there were 110,000 Mexicans, 4,000 to 5,000 Americans, 300 to 400 Jews, 15,000 Catholic Indians, and 30,000 unsettled Indians in New Mexico.[3] By 1868, registry at elections was required by law and daily mail service from the East was established. New Mexico was entering a stage in which an increasingly provincial attitude and identity with the region as a home gave rise to a working local political system. All these factors would have an effect on Felsenthal's future.

Once he was back in Santa Fe and a civilian again, Felsenthal was faced with the problem of making a living. Although he may have been, for a time, involved in "the mercantile business" as he mentioned in his letter requesting a speedy dismissal from the military, by 1870 his occupation was that of a claims agent.[4] He worked out of the law office of his friend, Charles Clever who, as an eminent lawyer and leader in public affairs, was able to maintain a very active practice. This, in turn, probably allowed Felsenthal to make a better living than he might have been able to as a merchant. Petitioners were filing claims against the territorial and federal governments as well as against each other as private citizens. Former soldiers who had never received all their pay from the Territory, widows suing for military pension benefits, claimants asserting they were owed reparations for loss or injury of personal property due to actions by the military or Indians, and various land claims, all combined to keep a number of claims agents busy in the Territory.

In the 1870 Santa Fe census, Felsenthal listed himself as a naturalized citizen and claimed personal property valued at $2,000. This amount was quadruple what he had claimed ten years before and was somehow accumulated even though he had spent a portion of that time in military pursuits.

At this time, Felsenthal was living in a boardinghouse run by a German-born painter—Edward Zimmer and his wife Jennie—who had been born in London. Four other men, all of German origin, lived at the same address, which was next door to former Justice of the Territorial Supreme Court, Joab Houghton, and his thriving family of six small children. The boardinghouse seemed to be a little Prussian island to which these men had gravitated when they found themselves adrift in a sea of Spanish-speaking Mexican-Americans whose culture, tastes, and ideas were so different from their own. The roomers appeared to be strikingly alike. All were apparently unmarried, or at least living alone, and all were in the age range of late twenties to middle thirties and held similar white-collar jobs such as clerks and salesmen.[5]

Felsenthal's choice of residence reveals something of his character. He spoke Spanish fluently, had chosen Mexican-American men to be lieutenants in his companies of volunteers, and had friends among the native population throughout his life; it would seem, however, that Felsenthal's Prussian-Jewish background, and the preferences and standards it had generated, made him most comfortable around persons of his own ancestry and perhaps was a factor in his failure ever to marry. During the earlier years of his life, when he would have been most likely to seek a wife, most of the available women were Hispanic Catholics. For him to have ignored his orthodox religious training and married one of these women would have been a very unusual action. A survey of forty-four Jewish merchant marriages in New Mexico between 1850 and 1900 showed that only five were contracted with Spanish women, two with Indians, and all the rest with Anglo-American or German women.[6] Some of the more affluent Jewish men in Santa Fe returned to New York, married women of their own faith there, and brought them back to the Territory. Others sent passage money to sweethearts in Prussia who sailed the Atlantic and came to Santa Fe to join them. But for some reason, perhaps financial, Felsenthal never did this.

Another part of Felsenthal's life is glimpsed in his choice of professional associates and the political machinations he was drawn into on their behalf. In 1867 his mentor, Charles Clever,[7] ran against the incumbent, Republican J. Francisco Chaves, in a contest for territorial delegate to Congress.[8] Clever, born in Cologne, Prussia, had come to Santa Fe in late 1849 as a bullwhacker for a freight contractor hauling government stores from Leavenworth, Kansas, and had quickly become engaged in merchandising. An ambitious man, with great strength of character, he began the study of law in 1857 and was admitted to the bar in 1861. He was active in the practice of his profession at the time he campaigned against Chaves, who was head of one of the most powerful landed families of the Spanish aristocracy and the former second-in-command of the New Mexico Volunteers.[9]

The political campaign was hard fought; there can be little doubt that Louis Felsenthal took an active part in it. It was seen by many as a power struggle between the Anglo faction and the native New Mexicans. The outcome was disturbingly close. Clever won over Chaves by a count of 8,891 votes to 8,794. The election of Clever was certified by the governor, and pro forma by the secretary of the Territory, and the delegate took his seat in September 1867. This had to be an exhilarating time for Felsenthal; his hopes for his future must have bloomed. Charles Clever, his friend and long-time champion, was now in a position of power and Felsenthal's life could be dramatically changed. But once again, as though dogged by a malevolent fate, Felsenthal's hopes and plans were to be crushed.

Territorial Secretary H. H. Heath made a separate certificate stating that the election was fraudulent, and this action of the secretary was endorsed by the legislative assembly. After a long and bitter contest, Colonel Chaves was finally seated in February 1869.

The *Santa Fe New Mexican,* a Republican newspaper that was violently anti-Clever and pro-Chaves, continually maligned Clever during the period he served in Washington as territorial delegate while the election that had put him there was being contested. In the issue of October 21, 1868, they reprinted a small item from the October 3 *Washington Chronicle* in which a reporter wrote about a disagreement between Clever and an ex-naval officer who had publicly denounced Queen Isabella of Spain as an unchaste woman. Clever apparently knocked the man down with his cane and the reporter conjectured that there might be a duel. In the item, the reporter referred to Clever as "a certain Spanish gentleman" and the *New Mexican,* unfairly, implied that Clever himself was telling people he was Spanish. In the caustic article, a classic example of the worst in partisan journalism in Santa Fe at that time, the *New Mexican* said,

Really, New Mexico, we should say, ought to feel proud of its *sitting* Delegate. Apostate Jew, and now a Catholic; occupying a seat in Congress that belongs to another, and at last abjuring not only his 'fatherland,' but the country of his adoption, and all of a sudden turning *Spaniard;* really, Clever is a trump of which New Mexico ought to feel very proud. . . . However, the mess of pottage for which he sold his religion in this country, he now enjoys. . . . we think it proper to say to our friends in Washington, to whom Clever is a Spaniard, that when he came to New Mexico, some fifteen years ago, he was a German of the Hebrew persuasion, and though he did drop off the mantle of Hebraic faith, we were not aware until the little affair in Washington . . . that he became a Spaniard by throwing off his mixed German origin.

Evidently the ousting of Clever as territorial delegate was the direct result of a bitter political battle then in progress in which Heath and the legislature had pitted themselves against the incumbent governor, Robert B. Mitchell and his strong advocate, Clever. The stormy hostilities began in 1867 when Governor

Mitchell declared that a number of laws, passed by the legislature during his absence from the Territory, were illegal and invalid. Legal backing for the governor's action was provided by Clever, his newly appointed attorney general, and after that a no-holds-barred series of political maneuvers took place, over the next several years, which were more typical than unique in the political arena of Santa Fe at that time.[10] The end result was Clever's defeat; thereafter his political power and public exposure appeared to have waned until his death in 1874.

Clever's defeat and accompanying loss of influence in both Washington and Santa Fe proved a severe blow to any dreams Felsenthal might have had for a notable career, for never again would he have such a powerful advocate.

A few months before Clever lost his post, however, the *Daily New Mexican* ran several small items which reveal another facet of Felsenthal's personality. Evidently Felsenthal enjoyed the "gentlemen's game" of billiards and felt himself competent enough to participate in a high stakes game, one involving more money than he had earned in a month as commanding officer of Company "C". On October 9, 1868, the newspaper took note of the event, saying, "There was a game of billiards of 500 points at the Fonda (the local hotel) last night between M. Kayser and Louis Felsenthal for $100.00 which was won by the former. We have not the innings, so cannot publish them, but we believe there was no run that exceeded that of McDevitt, recently at Chicago." Apparently chagrined at the loss, Felsenthal seems to have asked for a rematch and gotten it, although for lower stakes. The next day's *New*

Mexican reported, "M. Kayser and Captain Felsenthal last night had another set-to at billiards, 160 points, for $40 which was won by the Captain."

Felsenthal had other interests, however, to fill his nonworking hours and most prominent among these was his involvement in veteran's affairs which began shortly after his return to civilian life and continued as long as he lived in Santa Fe. Without a doubt Louis Felsenthal was present at the ceremonies held on November 5, 1867, to lay the cornerstone of the Soldiers' Monument in the center of the Plaza in Santa Fe. Even though most of the soldiers being honored were Hispanic Catholics, the occasion had strong Masonic overtones. Placed within the cornerstone were a list of the military officers who had served in the battles at Valverde, Apache Canyon, and Glorieta, copies of various territorial newspapers, coins and currency then in use, copies of territorial laws, and various other items. The ceremony was impressive, with speeches by many dignitaries, including the governor of Colorado who represented the Colorado troops who had been so helpful in thwarting the Confederate invasion. Surely Captain Felsenthal, resplendent in his uniform, stood in the Plaza that day with many of the other veterans to whom the dedication was being made, listening to the speeches and stirring tunes played by the Fort Marcy band.

The obelisk which topped the cornerstone was not completed until June of the following year. Its wording commemorates New Mexico's defenders against both hostile Indians and the Texan invaders. Strangely enough, this monument to Union forces is situated *below* the Mason-Dixon Line.

This commemorative service was but one of Louis Felsenthal's veterans activities. Part of his fascination with things military might well have stemmed from his early days in Prussia where soldiers, and particularly officers, were perceived as figures of distinction and esteem, replete with social prestige and glamour. But there was more to it than that. There was a brotherhood, a common bond, among the many men who had defended the New Mexico Territory in its time of need and this fraternity remained strong throughout their lives. It appeared to supersede minor quarrels, petty dislikes, and disagreements, for research shows that when a fellow veteran needed help, in most cases even those who had previously had a difference of opinion would come forward. Patriotism remained strong in these men, they were active in organizations like the Grand Army of the Republic, and many could be counted upon to turn out for various civic and patriotic celebrations.

In February 1869, a group of Regular Army officers and former Volunteer officers, desirous of starting a veteran's organization, published a notice in the local newspaper urging "all those who have served honorably in the Army of the United States during the late rebellion to meet on March 4 for the purpose of organizing a friendly association or society for mutual benefit and to perpetuate the memory of those who served . . . in time of peril . . . and for the purpose of adopting a badge to be worn on all suitable occasions."[11] Felsenthal was among those who signed the notice.

The March 4th meeting was held in the Plaza and nearly one hundred members joined the "Society of the Army of New Mexico" after listening to pieces played by the military band and the rhetoric of Acting Governor H. H. Heath and various military, civil, and territorial officials. Louis Felsenthal was elected one of the five directors of the organization, whose duties included the processing of applications for membership from other veterans who desired to join. Felsenthal, like many other Civil War officers, would be addressed by his rank as an honorary title the rest of his life.

There were other exciting public events to attend that year in Santa Fe, also. On Sunday, October 10, the cornerstone was laid for Archbishop Lamy's new cathedral. The third largest donation received, at that point, for the Catholic structure was the $1,000 Charles Clever gave. Another large Jewish contributor was the Spiegelberg family who gave $500. Bishop Lamy was an old friend of the Jewish community of Santa Fe; when they held their holy-day observances, Lamy was usually present.[12] The Jews in Santa Fe were cultural, social, and civic leaders and often loaned money for the construction of facilities for public use such as parks, hotels, and churches. They reportedly often charged little or no interest on such loans or canceled them in cases of hardship.

It was also in 1869 that William A. Pile was appointed governor of the Territory. Pile, considered by some as a political hack interested mainly in increasing his personal wealth through land-grant schemes, was an outsider with little knowledge or interest in the historical heritage of New Mexico. It is alleged that he, on discovering large accumulations of old papers and documents of the Santa Fe Archives in some rooms of the Palace of the Governors, ordered that they be cleared out and sold as waste paper. It is true that he did dispose of a great many of these documents from the earliest Spanish period in New Mexico, but whether they were actually used for waste paper is still a matter of controversy. Public appeals at the time resulted in the return of some documents and a few others were regained on several occasions later, the last turned in by a private citizen in 1886. Pile's actions, however, did indeed cause at least partial destruction and dispersal of the archives and raised a stormy protest among the people of the city. Undoubtedly, Felsenthal, with his great interest in the preservation of historical materials, was as outraged as anyone in Santa Fe. The anger of the people of the Territory over this and other actions by Pile was transmitted to Washington and many felt this was a factor in his being relieved as governor in 1871 and being sent to another post as minister to Venezuela.

Although it would not become common knowledge for another ten years, Felsenthal, in a typical action, had managed to secure several of the old documents and preserve them.

There is little information available about Louis Felsenthal's activities during the first five years of the 1870s which led to the suspicion, for a time, that he might have moved to Pioche City, Nevada, where there were several items in the local newspaper mentioning a Louis Felsenthal who served as a delegate to the state Republican convention and made a trip to San Francisco. Later research was to prove, however, that this was only a most amazing coincidence, for during the same period in 1872, Louis Felsenthal was in Santa Fe serving as post commander of McRae Post No. 1, Grand Army of the Republic.[13]

During that decade Felsenthal continued to follow the profession of claims agent in Santa Fe, even after the death of his friend Charles Clever, with whom he had worked so closely. Santa Fe County records show that Felsenthal applied for and received an annual license to pursue such employment on May 1, 1876. It would also seem that he remained an active and esteemed member of the community with a lively interest and involvement in the social affairs of the city.

Veteran activities remained a prominent part of his social life. The *Daily New Mexican* issue of May 27, 1880 related the details of a meeting of members of the Grand Army of the Republic and ex-Union soldiers to plan an observance of Decoration Day. Committees were selected to arrange for ceremonies, decoration of the graves of the fallen soldiers, and musical tributes. Captain Felsenthal was elected chairman and chief marshal of the committee on arrangements. Serving under him were a number of men including William G. Ritch who had earlier served as governor for a period and former Volunteer Major José D. Sena.

Shortly thereafter, on July 12, the *Weekly New Mexican* ran an article that described one of the highlights of that summer in Santa Fe, the visit of former President Ulysses S. Grant. General Grant had come to New Mexico to inspect some gold mines at the New Placers, situated at the foot of the San Pedro Mountains, about thirty miles south of Santa Fe. Although Grant was on a personal trip, investigating some private investments, Santa Fe gave him a royal welcome. Just five months before a branch line of the railroad had finally arrived at the city, and now most of Santa Fe turned out to greet the general and his wife upon their appearance at the depot. Committees, set up to arrange for the general's reception and entertainment, had planned a procession to take his party from the station to the Plaza where a salute would be fired and speeches made by prominent local military figures. Louis Felsenthal was accorded the honor of being appointed chief of the parade marshals. The festive procession was led off by a military band, which was followed by federal officials, then military officers, the territorial officials, various reception committee members, and the general and his party, riding in a carriage drawn by four white horses. Following the general's carriage were the college band from St. Michaels, then groups of school children, and finally, various citizens on foot, on horses, and in carriages. That night a banquet was held, during which Felsenthal and the other marshals led a torchlight procession to honor Grant.

During this same month the newspaper carried a story about Felsenthal headlined "A Curious Document Supplying Missing Scraps of History," which stated in part:

Captain Louis Felsenthal has in his possession a document which for its antiquity of date and the facts of which it treats teems with interest for the people of Santa Fe and the country at large. . . . Captain Felsenthal has been a resident of Santa Fe for 25 years, and is one of the best posted men on the history of the Capital and the Territory now residing here. He is and has been for years interested in the records of the oldest city in America, and when in 1870 Governor W. A. Pile committed his deeds of vandalism, and with a high and unrestrained hand, burned, sold and scattered broadcast valuable documents and public records throwing light upon the history of the Territory, he succeeded in rescuing from the general destruction several very interesting papers, among which is the one now in question. This document is a warrant for the arrest and execution of certain individuals convicted of high treason against the King during the first half of the 17th Century. It is dated November the 24th, 1643, and is signed by Alonzo Pacheco de Heredia, Governor and Captain General of the Kingdom and provinces of New Mexico. Now in all the records of the history of New Mexico there is no account given of the decade between 1640 and 1650. 'The Conquest of New Mexico' by W. W. H. Davis, probably the most complete history in existence being totally without facts concerning this period and ignorant of the name of the Governor and all other officials of that time. The death warrant, which fills this gap, was issued against persons mentioned therein . . . for having incited the Indians to rise against the Spanish authorities and having told and exhorted them to obey and fear neither God nor the King. It was written of course in Spanish and from translations made by Captain Felsenthal the *New Mexican* is able to give the text of the document.[14]

Louis Felsenthal's continuing interest in things historical and his foresight in realizing the importance of preserving them caused him to take another action that year. Twenty-one years earlier he had been one of the founders and initial members of the Historical Society of New Mexico, which had existed for only a few years before the pressures of the Civil War led to its demise. Now, he and several friends thought the Society should be brought back to life. Accordingly, in December 1880, the four men purchased an ad in the newspaper suggesting that all interested parties meet to reorganize the Society. Most appropriately, they chose December 26, the same date as the original meeting in 1859. An article in the *Daily New Mexican* of December 28 states that Gen. H. M. Atkinson, territorial surveyor general, was called on to preside and Capt. Louis Felsenthal was made secretary of the meeting. As acting secretary, Felsenthal was called upon to state the object of the meeting and read the constitution of the old society, which was adopted, after slight alteration, as the constitution of the new.

Again Felsenthal was involved with important men of the city and the Territory. Among the nine men who reorganized the Historical Society that day were General Atkinson; L. Bradford Prince, chief justice of the New Mexico Supreme Court who in nine more years would be governor; Territorial Secretary William G. Ritch, who had periodically served as acting territorial governor; Samuel Ellison, once clerk of the Territorial Supreme Court and now territorial librarian; David J. Miller, who for twenty years had been chief clerk and translator for the Federal Surveyors General; and Sol Spiegelberg, oldest brother and pioneer founder of his family's prestigious banking and merchandising interests.

The meeting concluded with a motion that a permanent organization be formed on the last Friday in January. At that time officers apparently were elected because, a month later, on February 21, 1881, newly elected Historical Society President W. G. Ritch delivered his inaugural address to assembled members at the Palace of the Governors. In it he credited "a published call signed by David J. Miller and Louis Felsenthal, members of the old society" with bringing together those who reestablished the Historical Society.[15] He described the location of the original organization as "rooms where the convent of the Sisters of Charity is now located"[16] and said it had remained there "until overtaken by the relentless distractions and wreck of the war of rebellion."

Society President Ritch's speech went on to predict a long and successful life for the reorganized society and he was correct; it is a viable and important group today. But one question comes to mind. Why was Louis Felsenthal, twice active in initiating the organization and a man both interested in and knowledgeable about the history of the area, never made an officer of either of the societies? No document or letter has come to light to show whether he declined to serve or whether he was deliberately passed over.

Felsenthal, nevertheless, continued to have a keen interest in New Mexico history and was an active member of the historical society, making various donations of personal items over the years. His fascination with historical documents, however, would have him embroiled in a court case within the next decade.

6

The Court Battle
1880–1892

Santa Fe in 1880 was a far different town from the cluster of single-storied adobe buildings Felsenthal had found when he arrived in the mid-1850s. In just twenty-five years, the influx of eastern culture and technology had made possible several centuries of progress in Santa Fe. Swept away was the almost medieval society, characterized by crude goods production, a polarity of social and economic conditions among the population, and a paradoxical attitude that combined devout religious beliefs with a convivial and permissive life-style. In place of the old ways had come a flood of Anglo-Saxon innovations both in technology and institutions. Now Santa Fe had some paved streets, a railroad, a telegraph, a few multi-storied brick buildings of Victorian architecture, the latest high-style dresses from the East, even a private woman's hospital, and now there were Presbyterian, Episcopalian, and Methodist ministers, private schools, the vote, and a court system and banks available.

In 1880, Santa Fe received its first omnibus; the town's water works was built; and in celebration of the new railroad, a group of excursionists took the train to Kansas, going and returning in only five days. It was in that year, too, that the Sisters of Charity, who had come to build, administer, and serve in a new hospital for the town, erected their convent. Upon the completion of the Santa Fe Gas Company that year, the first gas lights in the Territory began burning, freeing the populace at last from the dangerous and greasy lamps and candles whose weak and flickering glow they had depended upon for the previous three centuries. From the south came word that Albuquerque had installed the Territory's first street railroad system. By October 1880, one of the last hostile Apache bands in New Mexico had been overtaken after it fled to Mexico and its leader, Chief Victorio, killed.

By the following year, Santa Fe had acquired its first kindergarten and first telephone. On the last day of 1881, Louis Felsenthal, now forty-nine years old, was appointed territorial adjutant general by Governor Sheldon, who had been the chief executive only since June. The New Year's Day edition of the 1882 *Santa Fe New Mexican* contained an official notice of the appointment which said, ". . . Captain Felsenthal of Santa Fe is a man of much military experience and will fill the office faithfully and well, so that while it is to be regretted from one point of view that Captain Frost has resigned it is gratifying to know that the Territory still has a capable officer in the Adjutant General."[1]

Felsenthal, however, held the post only two months. On March 1, 1882, Edward L. Bartlett was appointed and commissioned adjutant general to replace Felsenthal.[2] The records show no reason for this short tenure. Felsenthal was not appointed acting adjutant general, as might be expected with a temporary assignment but, on the other hand, there is no indication that he was replaced because of lack of efficiency or ability. Possibly Max Frost, the new editor of the *New Mexican* and prominent Republican member of the Santa Fe Ring,[3] was anxious to resign the position for personal reasons and Felsenthal accepted it with the understanding that a search would be made for a more permanent appointee, for his successor held the position until 1886. Whatever the circumstances, the very fact of Felsenthal's appointment can be interpreted as proof that he was held in some esteem by the political factions then in power. The office, although always filled by a trained soldier who directed the activities of the territorial militia, was considered a political plum.

In March 1882, Felsenthal gave the Historical Society the portrait of himself that he had taken while on leave from Fort Union in 1865 and records of the Carleton Post No. 3, GAR, headquartered in Santa Fe, list him as a member in 1883. However, the next seven years of Felsenthal's life remain a mystery. Surprisingly, a census of all Civil War veterans, made in Santa Fe county in 1885, does not list him, raising the question of whether he might have left Santa Fe for a period of time for it seems improbable that Captain Felsenthal would have allowed himself to be overlooked if he had been in the vicinity when it was being taken.

Felsenthal was back on record in 1890, however, with a court case that pitted various former and current officials against each other. Felsenthal, a former adjutant general, sued Winfield S. Fletcher, the incumbent adjutant general. Fletcher's attorney was Edward Bartlett, also a former adjutant general, the man who had succeeded Felsenthal eight years before. Before the whole proceeding was over, Bartlett had moved to the position of solicitor general of the Territory and, in that office, had to endorse and approve the final deposition of the case. Such involved situations were not so unusual in Santa Fe in the territorial era; a few men had political control, and a small group of individuals shunted from position to position at the whim of those with the power to make appointments.

The central issue in the case was a number of documents, papers, and records of the New Mexico Volunteers from the Civil War period. Felsenthal, in an action typical of him, had found these military records interesting, important, and historically valuable; he then kept them. Although there were laws and military regulations in effect in the 1860s that stated that such records were to be turned in to the Military Department of New Mexico or the War Department in Washington, many officers had a cavalier attitude toward all such official edicts. Felsenthal, evidently learning on several occasions that such items were going to be discarded or destroyed, took them to save. In a letter in 1894 referring to these records, former Lt. Col. J. Francisco Chaves said, "It was certainly a strange piece of Vandalism for regular Officers to whom they were confided for safe keeping that they took it upon themselves to think that they were not of sufficient importance to have retained them . . . instead of giving them as a sort of a present to Louis Felsenthal."[4]

Apparently, Fletcher, the adjutant general, learned that Felsenthal had the papers in his possession and verbally requested that the records be given to his office; Felsenthal refused. On June 26, 1890, the items, along with some of Felsenthal's personal effects, disappeared from Felsenthal's home and turned up in the possession of Fletcher. Angered at what he must have felt was an intolerable action, Felsenthal turned to the law for justice. On July 2, Felsenthal posted a Replevin Bond in the amount of $100, with Justice of the Peace C. Martinez, and applied for a writ of replevin (or return of the items) against Fletcher. One of the cosigners of Felsenthal's bond was Bernard Seligman, the well-to-do Santa Fe merchant who had been Felsenthal's friend since his earliest days in Santa Fe. Seligman had been appointed territorial treasurer four years earlier by reform Governor Edmund G. Ross who tried, with limited success, to modernize and clean up the New Mexico political system.

Legal action had begun and the battle was on. Felsenthal filed affidavits listing the goods and chattels he claimed Fletcher had wrongfully detained. Included was a box of papers from the estate of the late John W. Dunn, for which he had been appointed administrator, another box containing a large "lot" of military records valued at twenty-five dollars, three boxes of personal sundries, a desk, and two paper letter files.[5]

Fletcher, by way of rebuttal and explanation, filed an argument with the justice of the peace stating that the court action should not be to determine which of the two men was entitled to the possession of the goods, but rather whether Felsenthal, at the time he sued, even had title or legal right to possess the items. Fletcher admitted that he had no claim to detain the three boxes of personal belongings or the desk and the papers it contained. Fletcher said that Felsenthal even admitted that when he had made demand for the return of his property, Fletcher had offered to turn those particular articles over to him. Fletcher, however, had refused to return the military records and Felsenthal had wanted all or nothing. Fletcher made no excuse or defense for what, literally, was theft. He did make a rather surprising statement in his argument when he said that Felsenthal had testified that he bought the military papers from army officers after they were out of the service and paid about one thousand dollars for them. It seems very unlikely that Felsenthal would have said such a thing because, in all his affidavits, he always valued the papers at a rather low sum. Fletcher's position was that the purchase was contrary to the laws of the United States and the Territory and that therefore, Felsenthal, as a private individual, had no right to the papers.

Justice of the Peace Martinez ruled in favor of Felsenthal and ordered that all the items in question be returned to him. Shortly thereafter, on July 24, Fletcher sent Felsenthal a letter in which he formally requested, as adjutant general of the Territory, that Felsenthal give him "a large number of the original Militia Rolls of the Militia of the Territory of New Mexico who were called into active service during the years 1861–1865."[6] Fletcher, now using legally and socially acceptable methods, went on to state that the "Muster Rolls and original papers such as General Orders, Reports, etc." should be turned over to him in his official capacity and ended the letter by demanding immediate possession of the documents.

Louis Felsenthal ignored the demand, so a few days later Fletcher filed an appeal in District Court; a hearing was set for August 5. Felsenthal retained an attorney, John P. Victory, and the legal maneuvering began in earnest. Motions were filed and quashed, writs sustained and struck, and affidavits amended and re-amended. In an amended affidavit filed by Felsenthal, he detailed the items he said had originally been taken. He listed two small wooden candle boxes containing papers, letters, receipts, and other documents belonging to the estate of the late John W. Dunn, which he valued at one dollar. Felsenthal went on to say that the Dunn papers, while in the possession of Fletcher, had been removed from their original boxes without the knowledge or consent of Felsenthal and placed in an empty champagne box, which he described in detail. He also listed, as taken by Fletcher, two small wooden or candle boxes and contents, which Felsenthal described as a large number of muster-out rolls and other papers and documents related to the Volunteer service of New Mexico prior to the year 1867. Felsenthal again charged that these items, which he now valued at only twenty dollars, had been removed from their original containers "by said defendant or some person on his behalf" and placed in an empty box, which had originally contained a dozen packages of smoking tobacco from a St. Louis company.[7] In addition, Felsenthal claimed that three large wooden boxes of sundries, containing clothing, books, and pictures, and valued at fifteen dollars, had been taken along with one desk with "all documents therein" which he valued at twelve dollars. The final missing items mentioned were two letter files with "old letters and other papers valued at two dollars." The list suggests that a person, lacking in exact knowledge of where things were kept, entered Felsenthal's rooms and removed anything which looked as though it might contain the military records.

Felsenthal was granted permission to retain the military records, which were now the crux of the controversy, pending the outcome of the case, on condition of a forty dollar bond, which he posted. Fletcher, dissatisfied with the ruling and showing great distrust, instructed his attorney, Bartlett, to file a petition with the court requesting that the bond be raised to two hundred dollars for "the safe-keeping and forthcoming of the property in dispute in this case."[8] He also petitioned for a return of the documents to him, stating,

that it would be highly detrimental to the public good, welfare, to have these papers and documents in the hands of any private person, awaiting the sitting of the next term of this Court, especially when such person is only obligated by a bond of forty dollars to produce or return the same and where they could not be reached for purpose of inspection, or taking of copies thereof by the parties interested, and where they would be liable to loss or theft, without any adequate remedy to the Defendant, or the people interested, or even they might be sold or otherwise disposed of, with no liability to said Plaintiff beyond the penalty named in his bond.[9]

Fletcher's concern at the possibility of theft of the records undoubtedly amused Felsenthal.

Fletcher's motion to have the bond raised was denied, and the case dragged on through the second half of 1890 and by the end of 1891 no decision on the matter had yet been rendered. On January 7, 1892, a trial date was set for January 15. However, on the day the trial was to begin, there was a surprising development. The governor, L. Bradford Prince swore out a legal document in which he said he felt that the sum of $500 was a just and proper one to be paid Felsenthal for the military documents and a full settlement of the suit. His justification was that Felsenthal had kept and preserved the papers in question for many years at his own cost and expense. It appears that the case was an embarrassment to the administration, particularly since its adjutant general was the defendant, but Governor Prince states only that he wishes to save the expense and delay of further litigation. Prince pledged himself to draw a warrant on December 20, almost a year later, to pay Felsenthal, provided the funds were available at that time. If the money was not available, he promised to recommend to the legislature at its next session that a special appropriation for this purpose be made.

Since Felsenthal had, before this time, turned over one-third interest in the papers and documents to his attorney, John P. Victory, as payment for handling the case, Victory was to be issued an order for $166.66 and a warrant for the balance was made out to Felsenthal. The next day the governor's agreement was sent to the various parties involved for endorsement. Victory signed, agreeing to dismiss the court action; Fletcher, the adjutant general, also agreed but was careful to insert the words, ". . . with the understanding that I, as defendant, was acting in my official capacity;"[10] and Bartlett, his former attorney, and now territorial solicitor general, signed, saying that he thought the settlement was the most desirable thing. His endorsement also provides the answer to how the out-of-court settlement came about, for he recommends ". . . that the offer to dismiss be accepted and the case settled in that way."[11] After all the endorsements of agreement had been obtained, Felsenthal's aptly named lawyer wrote to him saying, "I have arranged matters in your case satisfactorily and the Governor has signed the paper I read to you yesterday."[12] He then instructed Felsenthal to deliver all the military papers to Colonel Fletcher. On January 19, the case was dismissed in the court and the matter was closed.

Louis Felsenthal was not the only person, however, who had retained such records pertaining to the service of the New Mexico Volunteers. A Santa Fe resident named Fernando Nolan had 353 military discharges, along with other papers, in his possession and the widow of Maj. José Sena had documents her husband had saved. Felsenthal's case, however, had set a precedent. The adjutant general's office had learned, the hard way, that old-fashioned, high-handed methods were no longer effective. It was a new era and people were more knowledgeable about their rights and recourse under the law. Polite letters were now sent to Mr. Nolan and Mrs. Sena, expressing the adjutant general's interest in obtaining the documents for his records, and offers of payment were made. In 1895, Mrs. Sena was paid $100 from territorial funds for her papers and Mr. Nolan turned over his documents the following year.[13]

Apparently considerable interest existed in the Felsenthal-Fletcher case among a number of people who kept track of its progress. Only a month after Felsenthal turned the papers over to Fletcher, former Lt. Col. J. Francisco Chaves wrote a letter to the adjutant general from Los Lunas, eighty miles south of Santa Fe. In it he requested that Colonel Fletcher look up a General Order of 1862 "among the papers which you obtained from Louis Felsenthal."[14] He hoped to gain information needed for making out pension claims for Volunteer veterans who had been discharged without any formal muster-out documents. Again, in May 1894, Chaves wrote to the adjutant general's office detailing case histories of enlisted veterans who could not obtain pensions because of the chaotic and incomplete state of the military records concerning the Volunteers from the Civil War period. This was the letter in which he had complained that Felsenthal had obtained the papers from officers some years before.

Perhaps his ire was justified, but on the other hand, if Felsenthal had not retrieved and saved the documents they might well have been destroyed and the records left in even more incomplete condition. It is possible that very little information about this important military era in the Territory would be available to historians today were it not for the foresight of men like Felsenthal, Nolan, and Sena who collected and saved what appears to have been a considerable number of military documents.

7

The Faltering Veteran
1892–1907

Lieutenant Colonel Chaves and others were interested in the records of service done by the Volunteers
because of the recently passed federal Pension Act of
June 27, 1890, which authorized monthly payments to
military veterans of the Civil War who were invalid.
The illiteracy of many of the native New Mexican
soldiers, the inability of many of the non–Spanish-
speaking officers to spell correctly the Hispanic names,
and the general confusion of the times, had all combined to leave many of the volunteer enlisted men
without any documentary proof of their military service during that earlier period. This proof was necessary before a man could apply for a disability pension.
Since they possessed no personal papers, their only
hope of establishing their legitimacy as veterans was
through the sadly incomplete records of the Volunteers.

It had been twenty-five years since the close of the
Civil War and many of the former soldiers were now in
their fifties. Some, who had not suffered severe wounds
of one kind or another, were now showing the physical
effects of many of the hardships they had undergone
while on duty during the war. Long periods of inade-

quate diet, exposure to inclement weather, and extreme and prolonged physical exertion, endured when they were younger, had originated conditions now aggravated by age. Many men who had been forced to sleep on the ground, often in rain or bitter cold, sometimes for months on end, were now becoming crippled by rheumatism. In the press of wartime priorities, many illnesses had gone untreated or been inadequately treated, and the men were now suffering the consequences of such neglect. The country, with a sense of social obligation to these former soldiers, had now set up a system to aid them in their need.

Louis Felsenthal, now fifty-nine years old, apparently was having some physical problems, possibly the result of a mild stroke suffered a few years previously. He, like many of the other veterans, decided to make application for soldiers' benefits under the pension act. One month before Governor Prince was to sign the agreement in settlement of the court case, Felsenthal took the first step necessary to initiate his request for a pension. On December 17, 1891, Captain Felsenthal swore out a declaration, in the office of a justice of the peace named Becker, to the effect that he was "unable to earn a support by reason of general physical disability."[1] Felsenthal's two witnesses were Sol Spiegelberg, owner of a general merchandise store in town, and a gentleman named Patrick Brady. This action initiated a prolonged bureaucratic process. Four months later, in April, Felsenthal was required to swear out another statement, this time before a notary named R. B. Willison. On this occasion he amplified his earlier statement, saying he suffered from "a general nervous debility beginning about twelve years ago," which he claimed "without cessation has continued to this day."[2] He went on to say that the condition disqualified him from attending to any business pursuits. At the same time, a local physician-surgeon, John H. Sloan, swore out an affidavit in which he diagnosed Felsenthal as suffering from paralytic dementia. He stated that Felsenthal "had so suffered during the nine years last during which time I have observed him almost daily and . . . have recognized the steady progressive deterioration of said Felsenthal's physical and mental faculties."[3]

The term *paralytic dementia* is no longer in use by the medical community. Medical dictionaries, however, define it as an archaic term used to describe a chronic syphilitic condition, a kind of encephalitis, characterized by degeneration of the cortical neurons, progressive insanity, and general paralysis which, if untreated, is ultimately fatal. If taken at face value, this would appear to be a serious diagnosis portending a bleak future for Felsenthal.

The picture Dr. Sloan painted, while dreary, appeared to become even darker, three months later, when he completed an official examination form. At that time he said that "owing to his condition, he [Felsenthal] is entirely unable to work at anything even the slightest exertion is too much for his strength."[4] He listed Felsenthal's height as five feet two inches and stated that he weighed one hundred twenty-seven and a half pounds, "having lost 40 lbs. in weight in the last two and one-half years." Sloan characterized Felsenthal as "just able to walk around without assistance" but said, "the disease [progressive paralytic dementia] is progressing rapidly and will soon render him entirely helpless." He described his patient as suffering from insomnia and loss of appetite and opined that Felsenthal was entitled to a full rating for disability since "his mind is utterly destroyed." Then, paradoxically, in the same statement he reports that Felsenthal has *no history of syphilis* and no indication of vicious habits, two items the government took into account when determining whether to bestow pensions. In light of the contradictory statements in the affidavit, one might be tempted to wonder whether Sloan, who was twice mayor of Santa Fe, was not a better politician than physician. On the other hand, perhaps he was exaggerating symptoms in a misguided attempt to help Felsenthal obtain a pension. One possible explanation, offered by current authorities, is that the term *paralytic dementia* was often used as a catch-all phrase to cover a variety of conditions, particularly arteriosclerosis, or hardening of the arteries, which occurs in old age, bringing on senility.[5] It seems reasonable to assume that Dr. Sloan must have been using the term in this manner, but as future events were to prove, his entire diagnosis was suspect.

Early that summer, the various affidavits and statements concerning Felsenthal's pension request were bundled together and sent to Washington for review. There, a routine search of the medical records covering the times of his military service was done. It showed no instance of medical treatment other than three day's treatment for constipation at Fort Union in 1865, after which he was returned to duty. The claim was then referred back to Santa Fe for further investigation.

Things were moving very slowly. It had been almost two years since Felsenthal had initiated the request for the pension and thirteen months since Dr. Sloan had claimed that Felsenthal's mind was utterly destroyed. But Louis Felsenthal was still functioning and supporting himself somehow. In August 1893, as a result of the return of the papers from Washington, J. S. Laferty, a special examiner of the Pensions Office, called Felsenthal in to make a deposition in the case. At that time Felsenthal appeared to show some evidence of confusion. If it is recorded correctly, he gave his age as fifty-seven, whereas he was actually only two and a half months shy of his sixty-first birthday. In April of the previous year, Dr. Sloan had also listed Felsenthal's age as fifty-seven, presumably at Felsenthal's word, even though he was fifty-nine at the time. There was also some confusion in the affidavit when Felsenthal stated that he had executed his original application for the pension approximately two years earlier before the clerk of the Probate Court with Col. E. H. Bergmann as one of his identifying witnesses. Felsenthal was in error and Laferty realized it. The following exchange then took place:

Laferty: Are you sure you did so?
Felsenthal: Yes, I am sure I went before the Probate Clerk.
Laferty: Did you ever execute any paper before J. H. Becker?
Felsenthal: No. He was formerly a J. P. here but now lives in Santa Cruz.
Laferty: Are you sure you did not execute your application before him?
Felsenthal: Yes, I am.
(Laferty then showed Felsenthal the original application.)
Felsenthal: The paper you show me, I signed that. It is my personal signature. I know both Patrick

Brady and Sol Spiegelberg. I remember now that the paper was executed before J. H. Becker and that Brady and Spiegelberg were with me at the time.

Laferty: But you said you executed your application before the Probate Clerk and that Bergmann acted as witness for you.

Felsenthal: But I remember, since seeing my application, that I was wrong before and that the paper was executed before Becker in the presence of Brady and Spiegelberg. I was sworn when I signed this paper and so were the witnesses. They were both present when I signed and I saw them sworn.[6]

This confusion may have been caused by Felsenthal's physical condition or by a memory lapse caused by surprise at having been unexpectedly called in by Laferty. It is also possible that Felsenthal was mistakenly thinking of one of the many statements he had made in conjunction with the prolonged court case over the military records. But examination of documents relating to Laferty's handling of the case shows prejudice on the special examiner's part. There is no way to determine if there was personal animosity between the two men or whether Laferty merely felt that Felsenthal was not entitled to claim a pension, but Laferty specifically stated that he gave Felsenthal no notice of the investigation and justified not doing so in a letter he enclosed with the paperwork he returned to Washington. It appears unusual and unnecessary for him to have documented, in such detail, the conversation he had with Felsenthal about which notary had attested to Felsenthal's original application. It was a minor matter, almost irrelevant, since Felsenthal had not falsified anything in the earlier document and it was valid. The most reasonable explanation seems to be that Felsenthal had sworn a statement before the probate clerk in the previous event of the district court case against Fletcher and merely mixed the two incidents up.

As Felsenthal continued the deposition for Laferty he stated that he was, at that time, a clerk for J. H. Purdy, lawyer and claims attorney, and the man who had served as his lawyer when he made the original application for his pension. He also gave the dates and details of his military service and stated that he had resigned from the military on account of private business and not because of disability of any kind. He added that he was making the claim for pension "on account of general debility—general nervous prostration" and went on to say, "I do not suffer with any particular injury, wound, or disease except that. I am generally debilitated, weak and easily exhausted."[7] In answer to other questions posed by Laferty, Felsenthal said he had been medically examined by Dr. Sloan, stating, "I did not pay him anything for examining me nor did he ever ask me for anything." Then Laferty brought up the point that was to plague Felsenthal for some time to come. He questioned Felsenthal about his drinking habits and in reply Felsenthal said, "I drink but very little. I have not been under the influence of liquor twice in my life." To a further question, he answered, "I have never had any venereal disease." He finished his statement by saying, "I can prove by Col. Bergmann, Candelario Martinez, Sol Spiegelberg and most anyone else that I am the man who served the U. S. as alleged." Felsenthal had named three prominent Santa Feans as identifying witnesses and over the next three weeks, each was called in by Laferty to give testimony about him. Edward H. Bergmann, the sixty-one year-old superintendent of the New Mexico Penitentiary was the first to appear on the following day. Bergmann, who had been a lieutenant colonel in the Volunteers began by stating that he knew Felsenthal well, having known him about thirty-two or thirty-three years. He then said that he thought Felsenthal was captain of Company "F" of his regiment, which was incorrect, and described him as "a little short fellow who lives in town somewhere."[8] He then continued with a subjective opinion saying, "From his appearance I should say he is somewhat dissipated. I don't think he bears a very good reputation." Accompanying Bergmann's statement to Washington was a separate sheet of paper on which Special Examiner Laferty would assess Bergmann's character as a witness. Laferty rated Bergmann as excellent.

On September 2, Candelario Martinez, forty-eight, appeared to make his deposition. He was an attorney who had entered the Volunteers as a sergeant and had later been commissioned an officer. It is also probable that he was the justice of the peace who had ruled in favor of Felsenthal in the military records case for, although court documents show only the initial "C" for the justice of the peace, Martinez did indeed serve in that capacity for a time. Martinez stated that he had known Felsenthal "all my lifetime" and added, "He is a very small man and has lived in Santa Fe ever since I have known him."[9] When Laferty asked again about

Felsenthal's character he got a different answer than Bergmann had given. Martinez said, "His habits, so far as I know, are good. He does not use intoxicating liquors nor opiates of any kind so far as I know."[10] Laferty undermined this testimony by rating Martinez as unreliable.

Sol Spiegelberg, sixty-nine, was the last witness to appear. He said he had known Felsenthal for thirty-five years, since 1858. Spiegelberg, who had been acting aide-de-camp to Colonel Canby during the Civil War said he could remember that Felsenthal had been a captain in the Volunteers but that he had forgotten which company he had commanded. Laferty went back to the subject of the original application, which he had discussed with Felsenthal at such length, showing the paper to Spiegelberg and asking him if he remembered signing it and whether he had been sworn under oath when he did so. Spiegelberg verified everything about the incident, saying the document bore his genuine signature, and stating only that he could not remember with certainty whether he had been sworn in at the time. He said he had signed a number of pension papers and did not remember very clearly the details of each case. In response to Laferty's questions about Felsenthal's drinking, Spiegelberg said, "Louis drinks some once in a while. I do not think he is a habitual drinker. Otherwise his habits are all right."[11] Laferty rated the character of the venerable Santa Fe merchant, who had long been one of the city's leading citizens, only as good.

Felsenthal had sworn under oath that he did not drink excessively. Two other witnesses had given corroborating testimony while the third, who obviously did not know Felsenthal intimately, vaguely implied that his reputation might not be the best but made no allegation that Felsenthal was a heavy drinker. Nothing in Felsenthal's background to that time even hinted that he might be a drinking man. To the contrary, during his military service he appeared to have been one of the more temperate officers in the Volunteers. Records show that many were reprimanded or put into temporary quarters "arrest" for incidents of drunkeness while his record is clear. Laferty, however, not only brought the subject up but, in a letter he included with the depositions on the case which he sent to Washington, said that Felsenthal was a well-known character in Santa Fe and that "His reputation is not very good. He has been a drinking man for years."[12]

It is interesting to note that Felsenthal had claimed, in his various depositions up to that point, to be suffering from nothing more than a general weakness and a nervous condition. But Dr. Sloan had diagnosed him as irreparably ravaged in mind and body and Examiner Laferty added the stigma of long-term alcoholism. If these statements were true, it would appear that Felsenthal must have been in dreadful physical condition, obvious to the most casual observer; however, two weeks later there was a startling change in the whole picture.

At that time Captain Felsenthal appeared before a three-man board which gave him a physical examination and filled out a Surgeon's Certificate with their findings. This would be the official statement on his condition and would be forwarded to Washington with the rest of the evidence. The physical was extensive and thorough, and the results were in sharp contrast to previous testimony. It would appear that either Louis Felsenthal had made a remarkable recovery or there had been some gross exaggerations on the part of someone. The board's report stated that Felsenthal had claimed only a general debility and shortness of breath. From their figures, it would appear that Felsenthal had grown one-half inch and gained seven and a half pounds since his examination by Dr. Sloan. The certificate reflected a complete investigation of the patient covering respiratory, cardiovascular, skeletal, nervous, and muscular systems and found everything well within the normal range. In contrast to Dr. Sloan's report, the board stated,

His [Felsenthal's] reflexes are normal. This man seems to be a slow easy going person totally devoid of ambition. His mental faculties are good—he is master of six different languages and manages to make a living by translating. He answers all our questions readily and correctly and says that his memory is still very good. This man appears to be well preserved and muscles are well developed but he is absolutely devoid of energy and ambition. There is no general debility and certainly no evidence of paralytic dementia as testified to by a certain physician as per testimony on file in the case.[13]

The report concludes with the statement that the examiners found ". . . no other disability. No evidence of vicious habits. No evidence of syphilis."

There was, however, one unattributed implication in the report. It said, "He is said to indulge frequently and freely in alcoholic stimulants but of that we have no personal knowledge." Considering Laferty's position, which involved connections with the examining board, and his probable influence on the members, it appears reasonable to assume that he was the one who imparted the information. In his cover letter to the commissioner of pensions, Laferty recommended rejection of Felsenthal's application. On February 16, 1894, word came from Washington that Felsenthal's invalid pension application had been rejected on the basis that no pensionable disability had been shown.

The entire incident appeared to have been a twenty-six-month exercise in futility and raised more questions than it answered. What was the basis for Laferty's prejudice against Felsenthal and why did he libel him with the charge of being a heavy drinker? This charge was now on the official records and would be investigated again in the future, always with negative results. Why did Dr. Sloan, on several occasions, diagnose Felsenthal as being severely incapacitated when he was not? Was he exaggerating, in a misguided attempt to help a friend obtain a pension? It seems evident that he and Felsenthal were not in collusion for Felsenthal never claimed anything but general debility, which paradoxically was borne out by the examining board's findings when they reiterated that he appeared devoid of ambition and energy. Future examinations would divulge symptoms which, in light of modern medical knowledge, suggest that Louis Felsenthal may indeed have suffered a mild and undiagnosed stroke some years before, at the time he complained of the onset of his symptoms.

Louis Felsenthal remained in Santa Fe, apparently able to support himself somehow, but life could not have been easy for the aging man whose health was slowly deteriorating. He had not given up the idea of obtaining a veteran's pension. Three years after his first application had been rejected, Felsenthal filed a supplemental declaration for pension. Surprisingly, his one-time critic, J. Francisco Chaves, took the time to appear as a witness on his behalf. Felsenthal had apparently become a little more sophisticated and knowledgeable about the business of filing, for this time, instead of a local attorney, he appointed Allan Rutherford of Washington, D. C. as his agent. The claim quickly and easily went through and before the end of the month he had been granted the sum of six dollars per month for senile debility, or weakness attributed to age.

For some reason, the Washington bureaucracy decided, more than a year after Felsenthal's pension was approved, that additional evidence in the case would be needed. First, Felsenthal was required to give information about his marital status and he informed the Bureau of Pensions that he had never been married and had no children. Then the same procedures Felsenthal followed with his original application were reenacted. Several men, who had known him well for almost forty years, swore out affidavits stating that approximately twelve years earlier he had suffered an attack of paralysis, which had left him very weak. They stated that when he walked short distances he had to stop to rest and regain his breath and that he was incapable of manual labor. Dr. Sloan, still on the scene, resubmitted a physician's report in which he again diagnosed Felsenthal as suffering from paralytic dementia and Felsenthal underwent another examination before a board of examiners.

The examination revealed some deterioration normal for his age, which was now sixty-six. Felsenthal had lost all his upper teeth from pyorrhea and the doctors found the senile arcs to be well marked on both eyes. But his hearing was normal, his body well nourished, and he was able to read without the aid of eyeglasses. The examiners rather ambiguously stated, "Answers questions intelligently but there is a general weakness of the mind more than what his age would justify."[14] The earlier allegation of alcoholism was investigated and the conclusion was ". . . no indication of alcoholism, in fact, he very seldom drinks." Felsenthal was adjudged two-thirds disabled by reason of weakness of age and commencing paralytic dementia.

In August of the following year, 1899, Felsenthal applied for an increase in his pension, saying that he was now entirely unable to earn a living. His two old friends, Solomon Spiegelberg and Bernard Seligman, stood as witnesses for him when he swore out his declaration for the increase. The three old men, whose combined ages totalled over 200 years, must have presented quite a sight as they gathered together in the office of the notary public. The turn of the century was imminent. Santa Fe and the Territory had changed. The men were archaic symbols representing a vital and essential period of development that had passed with the coming of the railroad. In the last twenty years of the nineteenth century, New Mexico had experienced sizable immigration, which brought with it changes in her native culture and economy as well as further Americanization and modernization of her government. Felsenthal and his two friends represented an earlier period characterized by the domination of almost all territorial enterprise by the merchant capitalists who arrived shortly after the American occupation, as these three men had. They had worked and fought to bring stability and safety to the area, but their time was now passed, and New Mexico had achieved conditions which would lead to her admission to the Union in 1912.

In March of the following year, Felsenthal again appeared before the examining board as a result of his request for an increase in his pension. The physical revealed further signs of aging such as dry skin, flabby muscles, and a heartbeat somewhat weak but still in the normal range for a man his age. The report stated that Felsenthal complained of two things, both of which would be appropriate if he had indeed suffered a mild stroke some years before. He said that at times he found great difficulty in pronunciation in ordinary conversations and also that he remembered events of recent date but was unable to relate happenings which had occurred during the war. The examiners stated that they found no evidence of vicious habits other than the fact that he now occasionally smoked a pipe. This examination revealed the first evidence of the condition that was eventually to take his life; the physicians stated that, at times, his urine flow was very slow.[15] Based on the information contained in the records dating back to Felsenthal's original application in 1892, the doctors specifically checked Felsenthal for paralytic dementia, in its classic definition as a syphilitic condition, and found no evidence of it. The board recommended a rating of total disability and Felsenthal's pension was raised to eight dollars a month.

The one strong and continuing thread in Felsenthal's life during this decade of deteriorating health and diminishing capabilities was his involvement in veteran's affairs. Obviously the GAR supplied him with a desperately needed milieu in which he could retain social contacts and a feeling of accomplishment. He served in many positions—agent, assistant inspector, junior vice commander, and on committees; he gave speeches, issued invitations, kept records, and attended ceremonies through 1901.

How Felsenthal was able to exist financially is a mystery. Obviously the eight-dollars-a-month pension money would have been inadequate for all his expenses. Possibly he was husbanding savings or the money he had received from the Territory for the military records to supplement his pension. In September 1902, shortly before his seventieth birthday, he was still living in Santa Fe, for in that month he applied for another increase in his pension. However, before action could be taken on the request, Louis Felsenthal was forced to leave his beloved Santa Fe forever.

Felsenthal's situation must have become desperate. This was a time when social welfare and retirement programs were nonexistent; the aged were mostly dependent on the extended family to ease their declining years. Felsenthal, now an old man in failing health, was alone with no wife, children, or relatives to care for him. He was unable to work and many of his old friends and acquaintances had died or moved away. Bernard Seligman, Felsenthal's close lifetime friend, would soon move back to Philadelphia and, within four years, die. J. Francisco Chaves would have his life ended by a murderer's bullet at Pinos Wells, N. M. in less than two years. Felsenthal, whose nearest kin was his brother, Levi, now living in Cologne, Germany, decided that the answer for him was to enter one of the Old Soldiers' Homes established at several places in the country to care for the aged veterans. At the end of 1902 he journeyed to Santa Monica, California, to enter the Branch National Home for Disabled Volunteer Soldiers, which had been authorized by an act of Congress and built there in 1888. Prior to that time, five branches of the original U.S. Soldiers' Home in Washington, D. C. had been established, but all were in the eastern part of the country. Pressures had mounted in the Congress to authorize one for veterans in the West, and once built, the California facility was situated almost 2,000 miles farther west than any other branch.

Surely Felsenthal hoped for comfortable living conditions, adequate food and medical care, and a relief from the misery of isolation that would be brought about by living with his aging peers in this domicile. After all, by 1902, there were more than 20,000 veterans, mostly from the Civil War, receiving domiciliary care provided at the various sites around the country.

Felsenthal's request for the latest increase in his pension was still pending when he made his move to California. However, on July 29, 1903, it was rejected. Two months later another request for the increase was submitted along with a new physical examination done at the Soldiers' Home. At this point Felsenthal alleged that he ". . . now suffers from disease of kidneys, catarrh [inflamation] of bladder plus uric acid poisoning, and from effects of paralysis of arms and legs and general debility, deafness, defective vision."[16] The examining physician's findings, however, show Felsenthal's condition to be comparatively good for a man almost seventy-two, particularly when considered against the relatively primitive state of medical care existing during his lifetime. He had lost the rest of his teeth but his claim of weak eyes was discounted with the statement that his vision, for both, was 20/40. There was evidence of urinary problems but the doctors judged his heart, lungs, neurological system, and hearing to be in the normal range. The request was again rejected by the government.

Washington, however, seemed finally to have become aware that advancing age alone could be a debilitating condition that was pensionable in the absence of other physical problems. In April of the following year, Felsenthal's pension was raised to twelve dollars a month, based on an order by the commissioner of pensions who ruled that proof of age over sixty-two was considered as an evidential fact of disability. Three years later, in February 1907, a bill was passed that allowed veterans over seventy years of age an increase, and the following month Felsenthal's pension was raised to fifteen dollars a month. To receive this increase, Captain Felsenthal was required to fill in a certificate, once again establishing his identity and age. Interestingly, two witnesses who signed the paper were Valentine Herbert, who stated he had known Felsenthal for forty years, and John W. Moyer, who had been acquainted with him for twenty, proof that other old soldiers from Santa Fe had been forced to turn to the Soldiers' Home as a residence in their declining years. Also living there was James H. Morrison who had served as one of Felsenthal's lieutenants in Company "C". Morrison, who was the same age as Felsenthal, had been a miner in California before entering the military and after his discharge from the New Mexico Volunteers in 1866, had returned to California to work as an upholsterer in San Francisco. Like Felsenthal he never married and when poor health incapacitated him in the 1890s, he too turned to the Home as a refuge.

On November 5, 1907, Felsenthal turned seventy-five years old and therefore eligible for an additional increase of five dollars a month. The day after his birthday, the paperwork necessary to apply was initiated and on November 13, the increase had already been granted. Again, two witnesses were required to swear to his identity, but neither Herbert or Moyer did so, which suggests they had died. Instead, two other men, whose shakey signatures bear witness to advanced age, signed, each stating that he had known Louis Felsenthal only one year.

8

The Last Years
1908–1909

It would be gratifying to record the last six years of Louis Felsenthal's life as a time when, safely ensconced in a federal facility for aged soldiers, he enjoyed what a Grand Army of the Republic report stated all veterans should, ". . . real homes in which the veterans delight to live and spend their declining years, with those surroundings of comfort and personal freedom which old age craves."[1] And a casual visitor or tourist, alighting from the trolley car which stopped in front of the Pacific Branch Old Soldiers' Home in the early part of the century, would probably have been convinced, from outward appearances, that the facility was providing exactly this sort of a situation for the old men. An article, written in 1911, described the exterior of the Home, saying:

It is an exceptionally beautiful place. The grounds comprise some 650 acres of land that overlook the sunset sea, not far from the Bay of Santa Monica. These grounds have been subjected to the highest skill of the landscape gardener. Summer and winter alike, the spot is aflame with flowers of every hue. Great, splendid trees are there, and shrubs and palms. Shaded walks invite the veterans to rest from the heat of the summer day, and sunny stretches of pathways are there for their feet in the sparkling radiance of the gentle California winter. The buildings are large and handsome. . . . "[2]

This idyllic picture, however, was incorporated in an article titled "A Nation's Disgrace," which was printed in the *West Coast Magazine* approximately two years after Felsenthal's death. The article revealed conditions in effect at Sawtelle (a nickname for the facility) so shameful that they triggered a congressional investigation and resulted in major reorganizations of its personnel and procedures. Based on testimony recorded in the congressional investigative report, a typical day in Felsenthal's life at the Soldiers' Home can be reconstructed.

At 5:30 each morning reveille would be sounded and the old men, mostly in their seventies and eighties, would rise. Even in California, during the winter months, it was still dark and cold at that hour. The men were living in wards, fifty men to a room, in three-story barracks, and the official report stated, "In most of the wards there is one heat radiator in the floor at one end of the room, and above that, near the ceiling, an air ventilator, which draws off the heat almost as fast as it comes into the room. We found many of the wards uncomfortably cold, especially early in the morning."[3] If the men wished to wash up before breakfast, they were forced to use communal roller towels and if they wished a bath in the single tub available, they were not furnished with individual towels. In some wards, the investigators found that four towels a day were used to serve fifty or sixty men. If a man was not able to get to the general mess to eat breakfast before it closed at 7 A.M., he did without food. The men gathered in large milling crowds in front of the dining room before meals, waiting for the doors to be opened. There were approximately 2,000 men in residence and no more than 750 could be fed at a time, so the procedure was carried out on a first-come, first-served basis with several sittings.

The food was served on long bare trestle tables and, according to committee findings, was badly cooked, poorly served, of insufficient variety and quantity, and totally unfit for men of advanced age. No water was available during the meal, sugar and milk was put into all the coffee before it was served with no accounting for individual tastes, and the coffee itself was ridiculously weak, being made with only 19 1/2 pounds of coffee to 110 gallons of water. The report further stated, "The bread is generally heavy, soggy, and unattractive in appearance, there is a lack of fruits and vegetables, not only in quantity but in variety. There is a sameness in the preparation and a lack of variety in the kind of food served morning, noon, and night that must become almost unendurable." Everyone involved in the investigation seemed to agree that the diet was totally inappropriate for the elderly men and that "their years were being shortened" to save a few dollars.

John S. McGroarty, the reporter who wrote the article that drew attention to conditions in the Soldiers' Home, testified that the old men were served cold soup in rough ironware soup bowls and then were required to use the same bowls as containers for their "hog and hominy" and potatoes which were served from common platters. Each man was given one small square of oleomargarine instead of butter, and no second helpings were allowed. The subsequent investigation showed that less than fifteen cents a day per man was being spent to feed the men at the California facility while at the National Home in Washington, D. C., the amount spent for food alone, exclusive of food-staff salaries and so forth, was thirty-five cents per day. It was obvious from the report, that skimming was being done by those in charge and that special food and service was available to certain employees and others in positions of power, whereby they obtained the choice cuts of meat and the best of the fruit, with the result that the general mess suffered.

The despicable conditions, however, extended far beyond the preparation and serving of food and touched every facet of the men's lives. Total regimentation of the old veterans was in effect; orders given by the staff had to be obeyed without explanation or question. There were 662 paragraphs of regulations governing the running of the Home, many irrational or outdated, and even though they were not available for examination by the old soldiers, they were expected to abide by them as though they were young military recruits. The staff kept the inmates cowed by threats to "give them the gate" or discharge them if they complained or failed to comply with all demands, however unfair. In the committee findings it was stated, "There is utterly lacking that cordial feeling of esteem, confidence, friendship, and comradeship that should exist in such an institution" between the members and the staff. They found just the opposite condition in effect and bluntly said that the officials did not have the confidence and good will of the inhabitants of the Sawtelle facility.

The report revealed that many of the old veterans were forced to toil around the Home without pay because officials took advantage of a regulation that provided for "emergency" work to be done by Home members without compensation. In addition, violation of any of the myriad rules or regulations often brought about punishment called "being sent to the dump," which meant being sentenced to an excessive amount of a certain class of work without pay.

In other instances, when the men were paid for their labor, they received only one-third to one-half what was paid civilians for similar work, although they were expected to do just as much. The investigative report cited examples such as this: "For instance, in the matter of dish washing, we found two members employed who had to get up about 5 o'clock in the morning and work until 7 or 8 o'clock at night and who are paid only one-half of what the civilians are paid who work with them."

In every area of their daily lives, Felsenthal and the other old men were mistreated and made miserable by a staff that refused to do any more than was absolutely necessary to maintain the members. Although the public concern did not begin until 1911, two years after Felsenthal's death, the investigation made it clear that the conditions had been in effect for some time and certainly covered the time period while Felsenthal was in residence. The report, sounding like a chapter from Dickens, told how the residents of the Home were required to wear "dead men's clothing" issued to them upon the demise of the former owner, in a dirty and unrepaired condition, without being fumigated or cleaned as required by regulation. In addition, the men slept on iron cots with mattresses that were "thin, poorly constructed, often insanitary, cold, and uncomfortable," and without sufficient blankets to keep them warm. The large, unpartitioned wards, with fifty or more beds aligned side by side, afforded no privacy, were poorly ventilated, and the investigators felt that "the air at night becomes foul, disease laden, and productive of colds and other sickness." In addition, the senile, the alcoholic, the sick, and the well men were all mingled in the barracks wards so that the nights were always punctuated by the noise of inhabitants walking the floors, raving in nightmares, coughing, snoring, or tossing and turning. The men were left entirely alone from the 9:00 P.M. mandatory bedtime until morning, with no watchman or nurse looking in to see if they needed help of any kind. On occasions, men died during the night and their demise was discovered in the morning by their companions.

As a result of the investigation, the governor in charge of the Soldiers' Home was pressured to resign, the doctor in charge of the Home hospital was removed and replaced, and the committee recommended an almost total reorganization and transferral of the Home to the supervision of the War Department. But all these changes came too late for Louis Felsenthal. He suffered through the most wretched period of the institition's misadministration and died, in 1909, shortly before conditions were made public.

A clue to Felsenthal's mental capacities at the age of seventy-five can be discovered by examination of a letter he wrote in April 1908, one year before his death. The letter was written in reply to a request from the Office of the U.S. Commissioner of Pensions asking for the best obtainable evidence of the date of his birth. He enclosed his 1854 Prussian passport and requested its return when no longer needed. The letter is an amazing document when considered against Felsenthal's age and the prior statements made about his mental and physical condition. The handwriting is firm and legible and in the ornate style that marked the educated person of the early nineteenth century. The lines of script are straight across the page and evenly spaced and the spelling, punctuation, and form are all correct. The content is clear and sequential and the letter could not, in any way other than the date, be distinguished from those he wrote more than forty years earlier. And this was the man whose mind had been diagnosed as utterly destroyed sixteen years earlier!

While Felsenthal resided at the Old Soldiers' Home, his kidney and bladder problems became progressively worse. Although he was diagnosed at that time as suffering from nephritis and cystitis, an evaluation of his recorded symptoms by authorities today strongly points to obstructive prostatism, a condition common in elderly men that is still a problem even in this era of antibiotics and skillful surgery.[4] The condition is characterized by an inflammation of the prostate, which obstructs urine flow from the bladder, resulting eventually in uric poisoning. By June 1, 1909, Felsenthal's disease had progressed to the point where he was admitted to the Home hospital. Unfortunately, this was the hospital that the committee was to find, two years later, to be in lamentable condition, "very badly managed," and where "the surgeon in charge and several of the assistant surgeons were at times negligent of the patients," and where "insanitary conditions prevailed." Felsenthal was in the hospital for eight days and if his disease followed a typical course, as the poisonous metabolic wastes built up in his system, he would have become confused and euphoric, then lapsed into a coma, and finally died of either heart failure or pneumonia. His death certificate shows that he died at 2:15 P.M. on June 8, without a doctor in attendance, for the signing physician states that he last saw him the day before. Cause of death was listed as chronic diffuse nephritis with contributory chronic cystitis, a technically incorrect diagnosis in all probability. The following day he was buried in the adjacent hospital burial grounds which, many years later, were designated the Los Angeles National Cemetery. Today, Felsenthal's headstone is one of thousands of mute white markers that stretch, in militarily precise rows, over acres of green grass. Its brief inscription reads simply, "Capt. Louis Felsenthal, Co. C, 1 N. Mex. Inf.". Such a few words to sum up an identity and a lifetime.

Not far away the tireless Pacific thrusts its waves against the beach and the muffled roar of traffic on the San Diego Freeway pushes in to challenge the silence of this haven of the voiceless dead. It is a very long way from Santa Fe where, under a turquoise sky, fragrant piñon-scented breezes slip down from the Sangre de Cristo mountains to perfume the simple adobe buildings, created from the very earth they hug.

Louis Felsenthal was not a shaper of events on a large scale; however, he certainly was representative, in many ways, of hundreds of others who, as a collective group, molded the course of New Mexico's territorial history. Without him, and his many unremembered peers, the Confederates might have been victorious in their invasion, with resultant effects that can only be conjectured. It would also have been impossible for federal troops alone, without the aid of the New Mexico Volunteers, to have subdued the hostile Indians at the time they did. The securing of the Santa Fe Trail for safe travel might have been retarded for years, again with unknown repercussions. Even the Historical Society of New Mexico might not have been established until much later, had not Felsenthal and several friends taken the initiative.

But in addition to these specific examples, Felsenthal's life story, from beginning to end, reflects portions and facets of the lives of innumerable others of his time. He was one immigrant among the many flooding the United States from Europe in the mid-1800s. Whether driven by desperation or its opposite—boundless optimism in a brighter future—these immigrants were a special breed and quite different from their peers who would not leave the familiar and comfortable realm of the "known." Felsenthal was also representative of the Jew in the early Southwest, an important group that had much impact on the economic and, often, the political conditions of the area, particularly since many were well-educated men. Felsenthal also typifies the thousands of civilians who became volunteer soldiers throughout the United States during the Civil War; men whose lives were disrupted by the hostilities and who were thrust into situations that would have been undreamed of only a few years earlier. The postwar years of Felsenthal's life shed light on the activities and attitudes of Victorian America; the patriotism which made national holidays a cause for community-wide celebrations and the love of pomp and ceremony which was reflected in frequent parades, speeches, band concerts, and dedications of monuments so dear to that period. Felsenthal's last years' unfortunately, reflect the plight of the elderly in a time before social security laws and social welfare programs. Had he not had veteran's status it is possible he could have found himself in an even worse predicament, forced into a county poorhouse, the final setting for many indigent elderly Americans.

In a more definitive way, however, Felsenthal's years paralleled one of the most exciting and fast-changing eras in New Mexico history—the Territorial period. When Felsenthal arrived in Santa Fe, New Mexico was still a frontier fraught with danger and steeped in the Hispanic culture of an isolated colonial outpost. By the time he left, Santa Fe flaunted all the best and worst features of turn-of-the-century progress—from electric lights to Victorian architecture. The recounting of the day-to-day details of his life, the listing of the various career positions he held, the naming of his various friends, acquaintances, and peers and their roles in influencing the course of his days, the mention of the many events in which he participated—social, political, military, and economic—all shed light upon the specific conditions, mores, and occurrences that impacted upon Santa Fe's citizens during the second half of the nineteenth century.

Louis Felsenthal's character, as it is revealed in his actions, is complex. He was bold enough to leave his homeland as a young man and settle in primitive Santa Fe; he seemed orthodox enough to forsake a life of companionship rather than marry outside his religion; he was a literate, educated, refined man who had the self-confidence to thrust himself into the unfamiliar role of military officer. Felsenthal showed a stubborn perseverance in his efforts both to regain a military commission and to secure a pension. That he had a certain modicum of vanity seems apparent from his acceptance of minor honorary posts such as parade marshal, his presentation of his photographic portrait to the Historical Society, and his chagrin at his unexpected mustering out of the service after the Battle of Valverde. Sarcastic indignation was revealed in several of his military letters, but overall he seemed to be a conventional man. It will probably never be known whether a lack of drive and determination or merely the vagaries of fate kept him from becoming one of the leading citizens of New Mexico, yet he was willing to fight a court battle against the establishment, in the form of the territorial adjutant general, for what he felt had been an injustice.

Perhaps Felsenthal's most pervasive quality was his fascination with the history of New Mexico and his awareness of the value contemporary things would have in the future, if collected and saved. It is indeed fitting that, some seventy years after his death far from the mountains and deserts of his adopted home, his biography would be written as a representative New Mexican of the Territorial period.

Notes

Chapter 1

1. Records Office, Iserlohn Town Archives, Iserlohn, West Germany. Felsenthal's paternal grandfather and grandmother were both born on New Year's Day, in 1760 and 1769 respectively, in the village of Oestrich. In the period between 1800 and 1805 they moved to nearby Iserlohn where Felsenthal's father was born in 1805. Felsenthal's granduncle, uncle, and brother, Levi, all merchant-dealers, were prominent people in the Jewish community of Iserlohn, acting as representatives and presidents of the synagogue and school communities.

2. Ibid.

By what appears to be a surprising coincidence, another family of German Jews, apparently unrelated to Louis Felsenthal, took the name Felsenthal in 1807, according to a family history compiled by Rabbi Bernhard Felsenthal of Chicago, in 1891. The rabbi states that the family lived near Kaiserslautern in the Rheinpfalz, which was a part of the French Empire at that time and, in accordance with a decree of the Emperor Napoleon that all Jews in France adopt regular family names, chose the name Felsenthal. Cecilia Felsenthal Felsenthal, a member of the same family, wrote in her book, *The Felsenthal Family:*

My great, great, grandfather, Isaac, born in 1732, was endowed with the attributes of leadership. At an assembly called together to promote the good of a common cause, he answered "Isaac" to the roll-call. "From where?" he was asked. He proudly answered, "Ich komme uber Fels und

Thal," the translation being, "I come over rock and dale," "Isaac Felsenthal," cried the presiding member of the assembly—and thus the name was enrolled. A few years later Isaac Felsenthal was delegated to assist in assigning family names, and as he reserved and recorded Felsenthal for his own name, those who derive their patrimony from the same source claim that all Felsenthals are related.

In spite of Cecilia's suggestion that all Felsenthals are kin, records of both families as far back as the mid-1700s show them living approximately 125 miles away from each other in the western part of Germany and no suggestion of any connection has been found. See, Cecilia F. Felsenthal, *The Felsenthal Family* (Memphis, Tenn.: Goldberger Printing & Publishing Co., 1939), p. 42 and p. 13.

    3. Passport No. 415, issued September 13, 1854 by Royal Prussian States to Louis Felsenthal, Felsenthal Military Pension Records (hereafter FMPR), National Archives, Washington, D.C.

    4. Other descriptions of early Santa Fe have been written by Paul Horgan, *Lamy of Santa Fe* (New York: Farrar, Straus and Giroux, 1975); Josiah Gregg, *The Commerce of the Prairies*, (Norman: University of Oklahoma Press, 1954); Stanley Vestal, *The Old Santa Fe Trail* (New York: Bantam Books, 1939); and Erna Fergusson, *New Mexico, A Pageant of Three Peoples*, (Albuquerque: University of New Mexico Press, 1951).

Chapter 2

    1. Lansing B. Bloom and Thomas C. Donnelly, *New Mexico History & Civics* (Albuquerque: The University of New Mexico Press, 1933), p. 219. This illustration shows an original 1857 Santa Fe newspaper advertisement for Hockady & Hall, a firm which had the contract to carry the U.S. mail.

    2. Ibid.

    3. Gregg, p. 77.

    4. There is some discrepancy in the spelling of Charles P. Clever's name. Various documents and books show it spelled "Clever" and "Cleaver," often both ways in a single volume. Even the *New Mexico Blue Book,* an official legislative tome pub-

lished in 1882, shows one spelling on page 25 of its New Mexico history section and a different spelling on pages 120 and 121 of the Legislative Assemblies section. More information on Clever is given in Floyd Fierman's "The Frontier Career of Charles Clever," *El Palacio 85, No. 4* (Winter 1979–1980); 2–6, 34–35.

5. William J. Parish, "The German Jew and the Commercial Revolution in Territorial New Mexico, 1850–1900," *New Mexico Historical Review* 35, No. 1 (January 1960): 16. Parish also says that in 1859, shortly after Felsenthal's arrival in the city, Santa Fe had approximately sixteen Jewish merchants.

6. *Bingham's Bill and Report on New Mexico Slave Codes,* pamphlet (Washington, D.C., 1860), Henry E. Huntington Library, San Marino, Calif.

7. New York *Tribune,* Dec. 31, 1860.

8. Ibid.

9. Lansing B. Bloom, ed., "Society Minutes-1859–1863," *New Mexico Historical Review* 18, No. 3 (July 1943): 290.

10. Ibid. p. 301.

11. Ibid. p. 307.

12. Ibid. p. 260. For further details of Capt. Muñoz and the revolt, see Gregg, p. 97. Possibly Felsenthal donated the historically valuable items to the Society for safekeeping. The Civil War had started several months earlier in the East, and possibly he had enough foresight to realize that unsettled times were approaching for New Mexico. He may have decided by this time that, if he were needed, he would serve in the army. If safekeeping was his motive, he made an error, for with the members scattered by the press of wartime and Indian fighting duties, the organization slowly lost membership and was dissolved on September 28, 1863. Most of the assets were sold to pay the organization's debts and the rest became scattered and disappeared.

Chapter 3

1. Records Office, Iserlohn Town Archives, Iserlohn, West Germany. Until 1866, Levi remained unmarried and lived with his mother. The house they occupied was torn down in the 1920s. In 1888, Levi held the position of representative of the synagogue community and president of the school community. By the early

1900s he had moved to Cologne and the name Felsenthal was no longer listed in the records of the city of Iserlohn.

2. Carson replaced Cerán St. Vrain, the original commanding officer, who resigned after a short time. Carson, who was born in Kentucky, first came to New Mexico at the age of fifteen when he joined a caravan bound for Santa Fe under the direction of Cerán St. Vrain. During the trip he helped a party of American trappers and traders on the expedition to punish Indians who had stolen most of their property. He distinguished himself as an Indian fighter, mountaineer, and trapper in the next few years as he ranged the Rocky Mountains from Montana to New Mexico and worked as a hunter to supply fresh meat for Bent's Fort. In 1843 he was the the guide who led Frémont's expedition to the Pacific coast. They made their way through mountains in the depth of winter, struggling through deep snows, and before reaching the valley of the Sacramento the men were compelled to eat their saddles while the mules were eating each other's tails. Frémont credited Carson with saving his life and through his efforts and reports Carson was lionized when he visited Washington, D. C. Carson also participated in the taking of California from the Mexicans in 1846.

3. Henry Connelly, *Address to the People of New Mexico,* broadside, Huntington Library Collections, and *Address,* September 9, 1861, National Archives, State Department Records, Territorial Papers, II.

4. Fort Union was built in 1851 on a site strategically situated 100 miles northeast of Santa Fe near the junction of the Mountain and Cimarron Branches of the Santa Fe Trail. The fort was a base of operations for both military and civilian ventures in New Mexico for forty years, until 1891. Today it is a national monument.

5. The Maynard was used mostly by cavalrymen because it was shorter than most of the rifles of that time. Since Felsenthal was only five feet tall, he probably found the carbine easier to handle. His particular model, manufactured in 1857, is a rare one. It was a prototype and only 400 were ever produced and few are still in existence. It featured an unusual and exciting innovation, dreamed up by a Washington, D. C. dentist named Edward Maynard. In place of the existing single primers which had to be

inserted individually to fire a weapon up until that time, he invented a tape, similar to those used nowadays in children's cap guns, in which the primer charges were sealed at intervals. This tape allowed a soldier to fire rapidly because each time the rifle was cocked, another charge was fed up into position automatically. Captain Felsenthal's Maynard has been in the possession of my husband for over twenty years.

6. Morrison, who changed his name from the original Marco, was born in Hanau, near the city of Frankfort, Germany, in 1821. He came to New Mexico in the 1840s with one of St. Vrain's bull trains and remained to set up a sutler's store at Las Vegas. Until he raised a company and joined the New Mexico Volunteers, he had been active in the merchantile and stock businesses for more than fifteen years in northern New Mexico. He, like Felsenthal, was fluent in a number of languages.

7. Valverde, which translates to "Green Valley," had long been a stopping place for travelers who wished to rest at the spot, which had abundant water from the river, good grazing for animals, shade trees, and a small settlement.

8. William A. Keleher, *Turmoil in New Mexico* (Santa Fe: The Rydal Press, 1952), pp. 173–74.

9. C. P. Clever to General James H. Carleton, Feb. 21, 1865, Felsenthal Military Service Records, National Archives, Washington, D. C.

10. Hayes is quoted in Ralph Emerson Twitchell's *Old Santa Fe* (Chicago: The Rio Grande Press, Inc., 1963), pp. 385–86. See also A. A. Hayes, Jr., *New Colorado and the Santa Fe Trail* (New York: Harper and Brothers, 1880).

Chapter 4

1. Warren A. Beck, *New Mexico: A History of Four Centuries* (Norman: University of Oklahoma Press, 1974), p. 189.

2. O. P. Hovey, Henry Connelly, and C. P. Clever to Brig. General E. R. S. Canby, June 5, 1862, Felsenthal Military Service Records, National Archives, Washington, D. C. (Hereafter FMSR, NA)

3. Louis Felsenthal to General E. R. S. Canby, July 8, 1862, FMSR, NA, Washington, D. C. At the time Felsenthal's com-

pany was broken up at Fort Craig it consisted of 55 enlisted men and 3 officers. The optimum number for such a company would have been between 64 and 82 privates, 13 noncommissioned officers, 2 musicians, and 3 officers.

4. Ibid.

5. C. P. Clever to General James H. Carleton, Feb. 21, 1865, FMSR, NA, Washington, D. C.

6. There was nothing unique about Felsenthal's failure to be paid by the military. As noted on page 155 of Keleher's *Turmoil in New Mexico*, on Nov. 18, 1861, (the last month Felsenthal was paid) Canby wrote to the paymaster general in Washington saying that many of the regular troops had not been paid for more than a year, and the volunteers not at all. The Territory was so short of funds that it issued warrants promising future payment to many of the soldiers.

7. Col. C. Carson to Capt. G. Chapin, Aug. 27, 1862, FMSR, NA, Washington, D. C.

8. General Order No. 25, Hdqtrs. Dept. of N. M., Sept. 22, 1863, Arrott Collection, Highlands University, Las Vegas, N. M. A bounty of one hundred dollars was promised soldiers who enlisted for three years and who served honorably for at least two. In addition a premium of two dollars was given to each accepted recruit or to whomever presented him to a recruiter.

9. General Order No. 82, Hdqtrs., Ft. Craig, N. M., Sept. 10, 1862, Bound book of General Orders, Coronado Room, University of New Mexico, Albuquerque. No specifics of the charge were listed in the document.

10. Col. J. C. McFerran to Brig. Gen. James H. Carleton, Aug. 28, 1864, *The War of the Rebellion*, Series I, XLI, Book 2 (Washington, D. C.: Govt. Printing Office, 1893), pp. 927–28.

11. Ibid. Maj. Scott J. Anthony to First Lt. J. E. Tappan, p. 926.

12. Ibid.

13. Louis Felsenthal to Post Adjutant, Fort Union, N. M., Oct. 20, 1864, Arrott Collection, Highlands University, Las Vegas, N. M. The retention of Felsenthal's men at Fort Lyon in no way implied that Felsenthal was an ineffective commander. Not only did the commanding officer of Fort Lyon outrank him, he was also the authority who would issue the orders for Felsenthal's

men to leave the fort and return. His actions in holding the men there were highly questionable and probably unethical since, by doing so, he was jeapordizing Company "C".

14. Recruiting Machowitz for his company had been a real feather in Felsenthal's cap for the sergeant was, without a doubt, one of the most dedicated and experienced military men in the whole New Mexico Territory. The amazing thing was that Felsenthal had been able to recruit him at all, for several years earlier Machowitz had been badly treated by the military. Machowitz began his thirty-one-year military career in St. Petersburg, Russia, in 1833, as a seven-year-old in the Prussian army, according to his own account. In 1850 he came to the United States and served in the U.S. Army for six years, part of that time under then brevet-Major James Carleton. In 1861 Machowitz became a first lieutenant in the New Mexico Volunteers and fought at the Battle of Valverde and was later transferred to Carson's cavalry. In the autumn of 1862, while serving as a company commander at Polvadera, New Mexico, Machowitz ran into trouble when it was discovered that the paperwork and record keeping of his unit was disorderly and incomplete. A board of three Regular Army officers recommended that he be told to resign his commission even though he testified that the lack of an English-speaking clerk had caused the problems and that the military had, in spite of repeated requests on his part, refused to help him obtain a qualified clerk.

Machowitz spent $500 of his own money to pay civilian clerks to bring his records up to date before being forced to resign. In an emotional letter to General Carleton, Machowitz said he was "writing in pain and tears," that he "considered himself disrespected," and that after they took his commission away he was "going to my farm to take the plow in my hand before I will raise the sword again." Why Machowitz agreed to reenlist fourteen months later as an enlisted man is unknown, although Felsenthal stated in a letter that he had given Machowitz a sum of money out of his own pocket to enlist the man he knew would be so knowledgeable about military matters and record keeping.

15. Capt. Louis Felsenthal to Commanding Officer, Fort Union, Nov. 9, 1864, Arrott Collection, Highlands University, Las Vegas, N. M. Felsenthal, in spite of his short stature and slight build,

seemed to be a physically sturdy individual and apparently suffered no ill effects from this incident. In fact, according to his pension records, during his entire army career he only reported on sick call one time, for treatment of constipation. Constipation was evidently a health problem for the military men of that time, probably due to their diet. One set of instructions, given to Captain Felsenthal and two other officers who were detailed to make an inventory of the stores at Fort Union, specified that they were to pay special attention to the amounts of laxatives and bread on hand.

16. Laundresses were commonly found at all the established posts and often at temporary facilities where the men were to be stationed for any extended period of time. They often traveled with the troops, they received rations, and were paid by the individual soldiers for cleaning their clothes.

17. Capt. Louis Felsenthal to Lt. John Lewis, Post Adjutant, Ft. Union, Nov. 14, 1864, Arrott Collection.

18. One year later Col. Selden's body was disinterred and taken to Santa Fe where it was buried in the Masonic cemetery with honors on Sunday, March 25, 1866 according to an article in the *Santa Fe New Mexican* of March 29, 1866.

19. Jerga is a Spanish word denoting a thick coarse cloth. In the photograph Felsenthal can be seen holding a cane with a metal top.

20. Special Orders No. 41, Hdqtrs., Ft. Union, April 13, 1865, Arrott Collection.

21. Louis Felsenthal to Major B. C. Cutler, Sept. 1, 1865, FMSR.

22. *War of the Rebellion*, Series I, IIL, Book 2, p. 1230.

23. Special Orders No. 2, District of New Mexico, Santa Fe, N. M., Sept. 21, 1865, Arrott Collection.

24. Louis Felsenthal to Lt. George H. Pettis, Regimental Adjt., Fort Craig, N.M., Nov. 9, 1865, Microcopy #427, Roll 34, re: Walter Tompson, Special Collections, University of New Mexico library, Albuquerque, N. M.

25. Special Order No. 36, Hdqtrs., Fort McRae, N. M., Dec. 31, 1865, FMSR.

26. Capt. Frank Harder to Maj. Cyrus H. DeForrest, Aide de Camp to Gen. James Carleton, May 26, 1966, Records of U.S.

Army Continental Commands, Dist. of N. Mex., General Records, Corres. #3156, Ltrs. Rcd., NA. Harder reported that Private Felipe Gallego (sic) was shot and mortally wounded on May 21 by Capt. John Slater of the California Volunteers. Gallegos, a native of Santa Cruz, N. M., apparently had been ordered, by Captain French, to be present to play the violin for a baile (dance) and was killed accidently when Captain Slater fired his pistol in a dispute with another officer.

Chapter 5

1. Paul Horgan, *Lamy of Santa Fe* (New York: Farrar, Straus and Giroux, 1975), pp. 344–50.
2. Ibid. p. 320.
3. Ibid. p. 335.
4. A claims agent was a sort of bill collector who assisted people in obtaining monies due them. Some placed ads in newspapers saying they were available to help soldiers, widows, and orphans.
5. 1870 U.S. Census, New Mexico State Records Center and Archives, Santa Fe.
6. Parish, p. 129.
7. Charles P. Clever came to the United States in 1848 and engaged in merchandising in Santa Fe from 1855 to 1862. In 1857 he held the position of U.S. marshall of the Territory. He was appointed adjutant general by Governor Connelly in 1861 and also served as an adjutant on the staff of Colonel Canby at the Battle of Valverde in February 1862. In a report of the battle, made by Maj. Charles E. Wesche of the Second New Mexico Militia, he states that after exchanging a few shots with the "Texas Boys," "Adjt. C. P. Clever brought me orders from Colonel Canby to cut off some wagons of the rebels, which Adjutant Clever said were visible from the top of the mesa." Wesche said that by proceeding in the direction indicated by Clever, he was able to capture and blow up a number of the enemy's supply wagons. Wesche was writing to Capt. William Nicodemus on February 22, 1862. The report can be found in *The War of the Rebellion*, Series I, LIII, pp. 452–53. Clever, like the other men of influence in Santa Fe at the time, held numerous public posi-

tions. He served as attorney general of the Territory in 1862, was reappointed in February 1863, and in February 1865, and again in 1867 to fill a vacancy. In 1864 he was also made commissioner to codify the laws. He at one time had partial control of the *Santa Fe Gazette* and had a great deal of power in the local Democratic party.

8. Territorial delegate was the highest and most influential elective office available at that time. He was the Territory's voice in Washington, its lobbyist for patronage, troops, and appropriations as well as the consultant for Indian affairs and the advocate of annuities.

9. Ralph E. Twitchell, *The Leading Facts of New Mexican History* (Cedar Rapids, Iowa: The Torch Press, 1912), p. 411.

10. Twitchell, p. 400 and Calvin Horn, *New Mexico's Troubled Years* (Albuquerque: Horn & Wallace, Publishers, 1963), pp. 115–32. Horn details the many phases and facets of the controversy between Mitchell and his opponents. ¶

11. The *Daily New Mexican*, February 27, 1869.

12. *The New Mexican*, Tuesday, October 12, 1869, and Horgan, p. 416.

13. *The Pioche Daily Record*, Thursday, September 19, 1872 and Friday November 1, 1872. In the Nevada silver mining town, the other Louis Felsenthal was associated with his father, Ph. Felsenthal, in a grocery and clothing business. Research has uncovered no relationship between the two Louis Felsenthals and not the slightest suggestion that they were aware of each other's existence. Since Pioche City was not laid out until 1869 or 1870, the father and son had lived elsewhere during the previous decade while Captain Felsenthal was a resident of New Mexico. The Louis Felsenthal of Pioche City died, while still a relatively young man, on March 24, 1877, in San Francisco after contracting a fever in Arizona while traveling westward on one of several business trips he made to that city. A few months later his father left the town and opened stores in two other nearby places.

14. *The Weekly New Mexican*, July 12, 1880.

15. W. G. Ritch, "Inaugural Address," *New Mexico Historical Society Publication No. 1*, Feb. 21, 1881.

16. The convent was located one block east of the Cathedral of St. Francis and, therefore, two blocks east of the plaza. Ritch also

went on to say that the first society had accumulated a "large and well arranged collection of antiquities—specimens and documents, and a considerable number of books, pamphlets and written contributions" but that with officers and members of the society "necessarily absorbed in the imperative duties of the troublous times" they had no way to care for the valuable collections and that "they soon became scattered, and remnants were finally sold to liquidate the indebtedness."

Chapter 6

1. In a gossipy little item, the *Santa Fe Daily Democrat* of Monday, January 2, 1882, asked, "How does Captain Felsenthal like his new title of Adjutant General? The Governor accepted with regret the resignation of Captain Frost as Adjutant General. If the Captain's successor will prove as accommodating, he'll be the right man in the right place."

2. H. H. Bancroft, in his *History of the Pacific States of North America,* lists Max Frost as Adjutant General from 1881–82, Louis Felsenthal from 1882–83, and E. I. Bartlett from 1883–86. However, the Territorial Executive Records in the New Mexico State Records Center and Archives, Santa Fe, show Felsenthal as serving from January 1, 1882 to March 1, 1882 when Edward L. Bartlett was appointed *vice* L. Felsenthal.

3. A mutually agreed enterprising clique of politicians, lawyers, businessmen, promoters, and others who banded together to virtually control the economic and political life of the Territory. Their primary interest was land speculation, which became a major opportunity after the Civil War, and by 1881 their organization was so strong they were able to wield great power. The "Ring" was affiliated with both major political parties, and members often acted in alliance with territorial and federal office-holders and manipulated themselves into ownership of enormous land grants.

4. Letter, J. Francisco Chaves, Los Lunas, NM, to Col. George W. Knaebel, Adj. Gen. of N. M., Santa Fe, dated May 13, 1894.

5. *Louis Felsenthal v. W. S. Fletcher,* Aug. 19, 1890, 1st Judicial District, Court Case #2786, State Records Center and Archives (hereafter SRCA) Santa Fe, N. M. John Dunn was Kit Carson's interpreter and clerk. During 1854 and 1855, while Carson was an

Indian agent he described Dunn as a man of "steady habits, attentive, industrious, skillful, and more than a clerk." The truth of the matter was that Dunn was administrative officer to Carson and took charge of the office while Carson was gone. Carson, who could not read, depended on Dunn to handle all the official paperwork while he handled the physical aspects of the job. Dunn and Felsenthal were both members of the original Historical Society.

6. W. S. Fletcher to Louis Felsenthal, July 24, 1890, SRCA.

7. Amended affidavit, Louis Felsenthal, Aug. 20, 1890, Case #2786, 1st Judicial District, SRCA.

8. Edward L. Bartlett to District Court, undated, Case #2786, SRCA.

9. Ibid.

10. Winfield S. Fletcher to Hon. L. Bradford Prince, No. 2786, undated endorsement to Jan. 15, 1892 Prince ltr., Adjutant General Files, SRCA.

11. Ibid., Edward L. Bartlett, solicitor general of N. M.

12. John P. Victory to Louis Felsenthal, Jan. 16, 1892, Adjutant General Files, SRCA.

13. Microfilm, Roll #88, "Territorial Archives of New Mexico," Coronado Room, University of New Mexico, Albuquerque. Evidently Felsenthal's court case received some publicity because after it was settled and he had received payment from the Territory, others let it be known that they also had documents. Fernando Nolan turned in a group of 18 muster rolls containing the names of 1,628 officers and men, 353 discharges, and 16 other muster rolls which must have contained over a thousand names—and he was promised payment for the papers. Two years later, at the urging of the adjutant general, he came up with 19 more muster rolls, 411 discharges, and 7 copies of other muster rolls, In all, it is possible that he turned in papers relating to the service of 5,000 men, although some of the lists were "originals" that the Adjutant General's Office had somehow obtained copies of. The quantity of Nolan's papers, when added to what Felsenthal and Mrs. Sena must have had, serves as an illustration of the pitiful condition of the Volunteer's records prior to the onset of the Militia Rolls issue.

14. J. Francisco Chaves to Maj. W. S. Fletcher, Adjutant General of N. M., Adjutant General Files, Feb. 21, 1892, SRCA.

Notes

Chapter 7

1. Declaration for Invalid Pension, December 17, 1891, Felsenthal Military Pension Records, National Archives, Washington, D. C. (Hereafter, FMPR, NA).

2. "Affidavit as to Nature of his Physical Condition," Pension Claim No. 1080128, Capt. Louis Felsenthal, Apr., 12, 1892, FMPR, NA.

3. "Affidavit as to Physical Condition of said Louis Felsenthal," Dr. J. H. Sloan, Apr. 14, 1892, FMPR, NA.

4. Surgeon's Certificate, J. H. Sloan, July 26, 1892, FMPR, NA.

5. Col. Philip D. Stansifer, former commander in chief of the Armed Services Institute of Pathology, Washington, D. C., and Dr. Joseph M. Bicknell, Chief, Neurology Department, University of New Mexico Medical Center, concur, after examining Felsenthal's medical records, that the term "paralytic dementia" was probably being used in this way. They feel it would have been contradictory for the physicians to use the term in its classic definition and then, on the same form, state catagorically that there was no evidence of syphilis. However, since the Wasserman test for syphilis was not developed or generally used until the early 1900s, no evidence of syphilis meant only that no history of known syphilis contact was shown, no lesions or rashes were evident, and no unusual neurologic signs commonly associated with the disease could be found. It was not an absolute guarantee that the disease was not present.

6. Deposition "A", Aug. 23, 1893, FMPR, NA.

7. Ibid.

8. Deposition "D", E. H. Bergmann, Aug. 24, 1893, FMPR, NA.

9. Deposition "C", Candelario Martinez, Sept. 2, 1893, FMPR, NA.

10. Ibid.

11. Deposition "B", Solomon Spiegelberg, Sept. 13 1893, FMPR, NA.

12. J. S. Laferty to Commissioner of Pensions, Washington, D. C., Sept. 30, 1893, FMPR, NA. It is hard to reconcile Laferty's description of Felsenthal as having been a drinking man for years

with a review of his occupational career. Felsenthal had been a claims agent, a clerk, a merchant, a translator, a military officer, an adjutant general of the Territory, and had worked for and with two very prominent Santa Fe lawyers, Purdy and Clever.

13. Surgeon's Certificate, Sept. 29, 1893, FMPR, NA. Robert Carter, M. D., of Corrales, N. M., concluded after reviewing Felsenthal's medical history that a stroke could have left Felsenthal with some personality changes and the lack of ambition cited in the medical examinations, and that he probably suffered from a generalized and cerebral arteriosclerosis with gradual and steady loss of many cognitive functions and memory, as well as some motor function.

14. Surgeon's Certificate, July 13, 1898, FMPR, NA. It is interesting to note that, on this occasion, Dr. Sloan was president of the examining board.

15. Surgeon's Certificate, March 7, 1900, FMPR, NA.

16. Surgeon's Certificate, Sept. 10, 1903, FMPR, NA.

Chapter 8

1. Report of the Committee on Military Affairs, No. 1167, United States Senate, Washington, D. C., 62nd Congress, 3rd Session, printed January 29, 1913, p. xii.

2. Congressional Record, "Speech by Senator John D. Works," December 15, 1911, p. 397. The McGroarty article, which had appeared earlier in the *West Coast Magazine*, published in Los Angeles, was read into the Congressional Record and was also included in the text of the Subcommittee of Committee on Military Affairs, U.S. Senate, investigation of the conditions of the Pacific Branch National Home. See "Investigation of the Conditions and Affairs of the Pacific Branch National Home for Disabled Volunteer Soldiers and Sailors, at Santa Monica, California," November 20, 1912.

3. Report of the Committee on Military Affairs, p. viii.

4. Edward L. Johnson, M. D., Albuquerque urologist and Colonel Stansifer both agree that Felsenthal's symptoms as recorded on his medical records suggest this condition. The fact that Felsenthal survived for nine years after the first symptoms were noted indicates that he must have been a very tough little man!

Selected Bibliography

Manuscript and Document Sources

Arrott Collection, Highlands University, Las Vegas, N. M.
California State Board of Health, Bureau of Vital Statistics
National Achives, Washington, D. C.
  Pension Records, Individual Soldiers
  Record Group 94

> "Compiled Service Records of Volunteer Union Soldiers Who served in Organizations from the Territory of New Mexico," Microcopy 427.

> "Returns from U.S. Military Post, Fort McRae, N. M., June 1863–October 1876," Microcopy 617, Roll 710.

> Records of the Adjutant Generals Office, 1783–1917, Regimental Record Book, Civil War, 1st Reg., N. M. Infantry, "Letters Sent and Received and Orders, 1861–66."

  Record Group 393, "Records of U.S. Army Continental Command, 1821–1920, Fort Union, N. M."
  Territorial Papers of U.S. Department of State, New Mexico, January 2, 1861–December 23, 1864.
New Mexico State Records Center and Archives, Santa Fe.
  Adjutant General Files, 1892–94.
  First Judicial District Records, Court Case # 2786.
  Grand Army of the Republic Collection, 1869–1903.
  Muster In Rolls, First Regiment, New Mexico Infantry Volunteers, 1861.

Santa Fe Census, 1860 and 1870.
Santa Fe County Records, 1876.
Territorial Census, Civil War Veterans, 1885.
A. B. Peticolas, Sergeant, Co. C, 4th Regt. Confederate States
Army. Unpublished Diary, 1867.
Records Office, Iserlohn, West Germany.
Registry, Address Books, and Census, 1846–1920.
University of New Mexico, Special Collections Department
Adjutant General Records, Microfilm Roll # 63.
U.S. Army, Department of New Mexico, General Orders,
1861–62.

Newspapers

New York Tribune, 1860.
Pioche Record (daily and weekly), Nevada Territory, 1872–80.
Santa Fe Daily Democrat, New Mexico Territory, 1882.
Santa Fe Gazette (daily and weekly), New Mexico Territory,
1861–65.
Santa Fe New Mexican (daily and weekly), 1866–82.

Books and Pamphlets

Bancroft, Hubert Howe. *History of Arizona and New Mexico, 1530–
1888*. San Francisco: History Co., 1889.
———. *History of the Pacific States of North America*. San Francis-
co: The History Co., 1890.
Beck, Warren A. *New Mexico, A History of Four Centuries*. Nor-
man: University of Oklahoma Press, 1974.
Bloom, Lansing B. and Thomas C. Donnelly. *New Mexico His-
tory and Civics*. Albuquerque: The University of New Mexico
Press, 1933.
———. *Bingham's Bill and Report on New Mexico Slave Codes*.
Washington, D.C.: Government Printing Office, 1860.
Edwards, William B. *Civil War Guns*. Harrisburg, Pa.: The Stack-
pole Co., 1962.
Felsenthal, Cecilia Felsenthal. *The Felsenthal Family*. Memphis:
Goldberger Printing & Publishing Co., 1939.
Fergusson, Erna. *New Mexico: A Pageant of Three Peoples*. Albu-
querque: University of New Mexico Press, 1951.

Giese, Dale F. *Echoes of the Bugle*. Tyrone, N. Mex.: Phelps Dodge Corp., 1976.

Gregg, Andrew K. *New Mexico in the Nineteenth Century: A Pictorial History*. Albuquerque: University of New Mexico Press, 1968.

Gregg, Josiah. *Commerce of the Prairies*. Edited by Max Moorhead. Norman: University of Oklahoma Press, 1974.

Hall, Martin Hardwick. *Sibley's New Mexico Campaign*. Austin: University of Texas Press, 1960.

Hart, Herbert M. *Old Forts of the Southwest*. New York: Bonanza Books, 1964.

Hertzog, Peter. *La Fonda: The Inn of Santa Fe*. Portales, N. Mex.: Bishop Printing & Litho. Co., 1962.

Horgan, Paul. *Lamy of Santa Fe*. New York: Farrar, Straus and Giroux, 1975.

Horn, Calvin. *New Mexico's Troubled Years*. Albuquerque: Horn & Wallace, 1963.

Ickis, Alonzo Ferdinand. *Bloody Trails Along the Rio Grande*. Denver: Old West Publishing Co., 1958.

Jenkins, Myra Ellen and Albert H. Schroeder. *A Brief History of New Mexico*. Albuquerque: University of New Mexico Press, 1974.

Keleher, William A. *Turmoil in New Mexico*. Santa Fe: Rydal Press, 1952.

Lamar, Howard Roberts. *The Far Southwest, 1846–1912*. New York: W. W. Norton & Co., 1970.

Magoffin, Susan Shelby. *Down the Santa Fe Trail and into Mexico*. Edited by Stella M. Drumm. New Haven: Yale University Press, 1962.

Oliva, Leo E. *Soldiers on the Santa Fe Trail*. Norman: University of Oklahoma Press, 1967.

Ritch, W. G., comp. *The New Mexico Blue Book*. Facsimile edition. Albuquerque: University of New Mexico Press, 1968.

Rywell, Martin. *United States Military Muskets, Rifles, Carbines and their Current Prices*. Union City, Tenn.: Pioneer Press, 1963.

Segale, Sister Blandina. *At the End of the Santa Fe Trail*. Milwaukee: The Bruce Publishing Co., 1949.

Taylor, Morris F. *First Mail West*. Albuquerque: University of New Mexico Press, 1971.

Twitchell, Ralph Emerson. *The Leading Facts of New Mexican History*, Vol. 2. Cedar Rapids: Torch Press, 1912.
————. *Old Santa Fe: The Story of New Mexico's Ancient Capital.* Reprint. Chicago: Rio Grande Press, 1963.
Utley, Robert M. *Fort Union National Monument, New Mexico.* Washington, D.C.: Government Printing Office, 1962.
Vestal, Stanley. *The Old Santa Fe Trail.* New York: Bantam Books, 1957.
The War of the Rebellion, A Compilation of the Official Records of the Union and Confederate Armies. Series I, XLI, and LIII. Washington, D.C.: Government Printing Office, 1880.

Articles

Bloom, Lansing B. ed. "Society Minutes, 1859–63," *New Mexico Historical Review* 18 (July 1943): 250–72.
Fierman, Floyd. "The Frontier Career of Charles Clever," *El Palacio* 85 (winter 1979–80): 2–6 and 34–35.
"First High Holy Days in New Mexico," *Western States Jewish Historical Quarterly* 7 (April 1975): 284.
McGroarty, John S. "A Nation's Disgrace," *West Coast Magazine* 1911, read into the *Congressional Record* by Sen. John D. Works, December 15, 1911, p. 397.
Parish, William J. "The German Jew and the Commercial Revolution in Territorial New Mexico, 1850–1900," *New Mexico Historical Review* 35 (January 1960): 1–29 and 129–50.
Ritch, W. G. "Inaugural Address," *New Mexico Historical Society Publication No. 1* (February 1881).

INDEX